WALKING IN UMBRIA

About the Author

Gillian Price was born in England but moved to Australia when young. After taking a degree in anthropology and working in adult education, she set off to travel through Asia and trek the Himalayas. The culmination of her journey was Venice where, her enthusiasm fired for mountains, the next logical step was towards the Dolomites, only hours away. Starting there, Gillian is steadily exploring the mountain ranges and flatter bits of Italy and bringing them to life for visitors in a series of outstanding guides for Cicerone.

When not out walking with Nicola, her Venetian cartographer husband, Gillian works as a freelance travel writer (www.gillianprice.eu). An adamant promoter of public transport to minimise environmental impact, she is an active member of the Italian Alpine Club CAI and Mountain Wilderness.

Other Cicerone guides by the author

Across the Eastern Alps – the E5
Alpine Flowers
Gran Paradiso: Alta Via 2 Trek and
   Day Walks
Italy's Sibillini National Park
Italy's Stelvio National Park
Shorter Walks in the Dolomites
Through the Italian Alps – the GTA
Tour of the Bernina
Trekking in the Apennines –
   the GEA
Trekking in the Dolomites

Walking and Trekking on Corfu
Walking on the Amalfi Coast
Walking in the Central Italian Alps
Walking on Corsica
Walking in the Dolomites
Walks and Treks in the
   Maritime Alps
Walking in Sicily
Walking in Tuscany
Walking Lake Como and Maggiore
Walking Lake Garda and Iseo

WALKING IN UMBRIA

by Gillian Price

CICERONE

JUNIPER HOUSE, MURLEY MOSS,
OXENHOLME ROAD, KENDAL, CUMBRIA LA9 7RL
www.cicerone.co.uk

© Gillian Price 2019
Second edition 2019
ISBN: 978 1 85284 966 5
First edition 2014

Printed by KHL Printing, Singapore.
A catalogue record for this book is available from the British Library.
All photographs are by the author unless otherwise stated.

Acknowledgments

For their help and maps, I would like to thank Tourist Offices throughout Umbria: Assisi, Cascia, Castiglione del Lago, Città di Castello, Foligno, Gubbio, Orvieto, Perugia, Spoleto, along with the Comune di Todi (Marco Spaccatini), Paolo Capocci for ex Spoleto–Norcia railway and Umbria branches of the Italian Alpine Club CAI – especially Luigino of Gubbio.

On the trail I enjoyed the enthusiastic company of Marty, Lucy and Clive who doubled as chauffeurs. Nicola kept the jokes coming, and did more of his marvellous maps. Grazie mille! This is a guidebook I didn't want to finish, as researching it was my excuse to return to glorious Umbria to seek out yet another 'unknown' valley.

Updates to this Guide

While every effort is made by our authors to ensure the accuracy of guidebooks as they go to print, changes can occur during the lifetime of an edition. Any updates that we know of for this guide will be on the Cicerone website (www.cicerone.co.uk/966/updates), so please check before planning your trip. We also advise that you check information about such things as transport, accommodation and shops locally. Even rights of way can be altered over time. We are always grateful for information about any discrepancies between a guidebook and the facts on the ground, sent by email to updates@cicerone.co.uk or by post to Cicerone, Juniper House, Murley Moss, Oxenholme Road, Kendal LA9 7RL.

Register your book: To sign up to receive free updates, special offers and GPX files where available, register your book at www.cicerone.co.uk.

Front cover: One of the well-established vineyards near Montefalco

CONTENTS

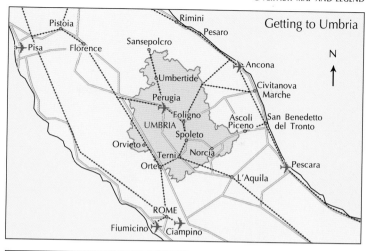

Getting to Umbria

N

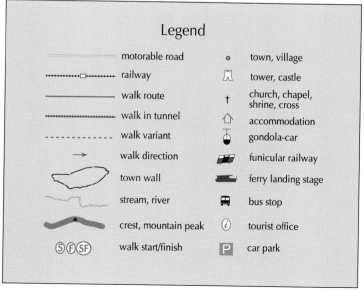

Legend

motorable road		⊙	town, village
railway		🏰	tower, castle
walk route		†	church, chapel, shrine, cross
walk in tunnel		⌂	accommodation
walk variant		🚡	gondola-car
walk direction		🚃	funicular railway
town wall		⛴	ferry landing stage
stream, river		🚌	bus stop
crest, mountain peak		ⓘ	tourist office
Ⓢ Ⓕ Ⓢ̵Ⓕ walk start/finish		P	car park

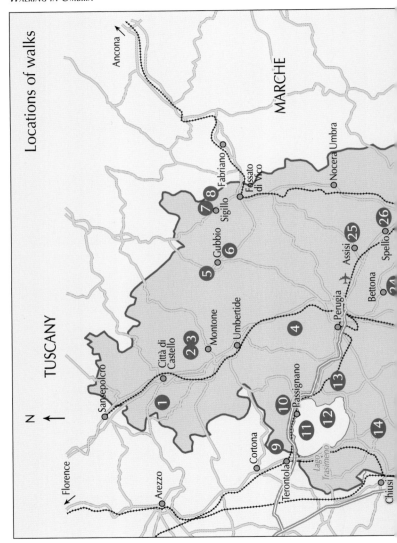

Locations of walks

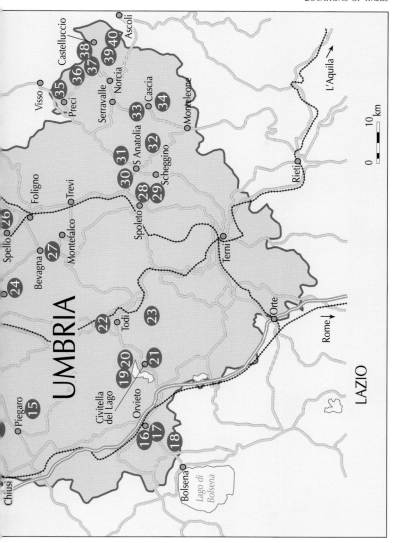

Ascoli

L'Aquila →

Castelluccio

39 40
36 38
37

35

Visso

Preci

Serravalle

Norcia

Cascia

33

34

Monteleone

S Anatolia

32

30 31

Scheggino

Rieti

Foligno

Trevi

28
29

26

Spoleto

Montefalco

Spello

27

Bevagna

24

UMBRIA

Terni

22
Todi

23

Orte

Rome ↓

Piegaro

15

19 20
21

LAZIO

Civitella
del Lago

Orvieto

16
17
18

Chiusi

Bolsena

Lago di
Bolsena

0   10
km

Eroding rock layers en route to Monte Gengarella (Walk 3)

INTRODUCTION

Vallo di Nera sits above wooded Valnerina (Walk 31)

Landlocked Umbria, with its array of fabulous landscapes, inspirational for so many artists and writers over the years, is rightly celebrated as the 'green heart' of Italy. Rolling hills swathed in dense woods, hilltop after marvellous hilltop occupied by charming walled villages which time seems to have left untouched. This region has much to offer outdoor enthusiasts, with superb walking guaranteed year-round on hundreds of kilometres of marked paths. These routes can be enjoyed in peace and quiet, for week upon week of memorable holidaying. They lead through beautifully cared for olive groves, along romantic river valleys, and explore regional and national parks alive with animal and bird life and masses of brilliant wildflowers. There is something for everyone – relaxing strolls for novice walkers through medieval and Renaissance villages and towns, flat routes around lakes and islands, as well as mildly strenuous paths to Apennine mountaintops and breathtaking viewpoints.

More good news? Life proceeds at a gentle pace in Umbria, which has little of the crowds and higher prices of its neighbour Tuscany. This is the first English-language walking guide to provide a comprehensive coverage of the walking possibilities, with a selection of 40 circular and one-way itineraries. The walks are clustered around the Unesco World Heritage towns of Assisi, Spoleto, Gubbio, Perugia, Norcia and Orvieto, each one a treasure trove of exquisite art works from the medieval and Renaissance times, as well as an excellent holiday base well served by public transport.

Umbria inspires great passion and affection, and visitors who take time out to explore this enchanting countryside on foot are sure to be captivated by its magic and want to come back time and time again. Be warned!

A POTTED HISTORY

Visitors to Umbria will encounter scores of reminders of the region's long and varied history in towns and across the countryside. The ancient tribe of the Umbri were the first recorded literate inhabitants of the region, probably around the 12th century BC. The more sophisticated Etruscans came next, leaving a fascinating heritage of necropolises or 'cities of the dead', and sophisticated craftwork (excellent examples of which can be admired in Orvieto).

The Romans fought their way onto the scene in 295BC and proceeded to play a decisive part in shaping the region. Road builders par excellence, they opened up access to and around Umbria by building the Via Flaminia, the Via Amerina-Tiberina and the Via Orvietana. Original paving stones are still visible at staging-post towns. Aqueducts (at Spello) and monumental theatres (at Gubbio) are also easily recognised as Roman.

As elsewhere, the end of peace and prosperity was marked by the decline of Roman domination and raids by 'barbarians' such as Huns and Goths passing through. The territory became fragmented, plague and famine rife, and local feudal systems took over, until the 6th-century invasion of the enlightened Lombards. Medieval times were characterised by the establishment of numerous so-called *comuni* or independent city states such as Spoleto and Assisi. Landmark town buildings date back to this period as do the heavy fortifications. Local skirmishes were the order of the day.

From the 1200s the comuni were gradually taken over and incorporated into the great conglomeration of the Papal states. This lasted through the Renaissance – when art and architecture flourished and the immense *rocca* forts (such as the one in Spoleto) were built – and up to the arrival of the French and Napoleon at the dawn of the 19th century. Not long afterwards, the great Italian patriot Giuseppe Garibaldi and his troops swept through on their northward campaign to free Italy of foreign domination, resulting in the unification of the country as the Kingdom of Italy in 1861.

PLANTS AND FLOWERS

A fascinating array of plants and flowers, both Mediterranean and alpine, is there to be admired from

Clockwise from top left: rock roses; poppies clustered under olive trees; the fruit and blossom of the strawberry tree; curious eryngo.

spring all the way through to autumn. Look out for wild asparagus, whose tender springtime tips are prized for sautéeing; at a later stage the plant becomes prickly and straggly. Curious giant fennel plants known as *ferula* produce bright green feathery leaves in spring, before shooting up a metre or so in summer. April and May will mean meadows of crocus and squill, primroses, cowslips, green hellebore and violets. As summer arrives one of the best places to catch a colourful display is the Piano Grande di Castelluccio, which will be ablaze with lemon yellow mustard, brilliant blue cornflowers, gay red poppies, campanulas, yellow gentians, scented pinks and thrift.

Attentive walkers will spot the exquisite insect orchids, as well as the more common larger purple and yellow varieties. One curious find is the bizarre orchid look-alike broomrape, a parasite lacking green pigment that has rich golden-red or pale yellow flowers and stalk.

Aromatic herbs are widespread, and walkers will be treated to the perfume of wild mint or thyme releasing their delicious smell when they are trampled by boots. Everlasting, a silvery plant with leaves like conifer needles and a delicious curry smell, sports a yellow flower head and is found on dry sunny terrain and crannies in stone walls. Its habitat is shared by delicate paper-like rock roses in rainbow hues.

Flourishing vineyards

The Mediterranean shrub and tree types commonly encountered include tree heather, which grows several metres tall, sports pretty clusters of tiny white bells and is gathered in late summer for use as brooms for street sweepers. A smaller species of heather has red-purple flowers. Heavenly scented yellow broom is common in early summer as is the attractive smoke bush with its fluffy orange blossoms in autumn. The peculiar so-called strawberry tree is widespread: glossy green leaves accompany both delicate creamy bellflowers and fruit at the same time. The latter are small nutty globes that turn red when ripe – however, as a taste will confirm, one is enough – as suggested by the Latin name *Arbutus unedo* 'eat one'.

A native to the Mediterranean region, *Quercus ilex* or holm or holly oak, is a large evergreen tree with a dense foliage of dark green leaves that are slightly toothed and have light grey undersides. Another omnipresent tree that needs little introduction is the cypress. Slender and pencil thin, it lines many an avenue and is silhouetted on many a ridge. A native of the Middle East, it was reputedly introduced to Italy by the Etruscans as the fragrant, knotty wood was prized for storage chests. One gigantic specimen – 30m tall and with a 2.45m girth – can be admired in the hill town of Todi: it was planted in 1849 to honour Giuseppe Garibaldi and is reputedly the world's tallest.

An autumn flowering marvel is field dweller eryngo, spiky globes with outstretched thistly leaves and stems stained bright mauve; another is the tiny exquisite cyclamen, which brightens up shady woodland. A less common aromatic is the bushy winter savory plant which flourishes in clearings and produces delicate white-lilac blooms long after summer has finished.

Autumn walkers will also notice weird and wonderful funghi sprouting in woodland undergrowth and on tree trunks. While many are edible and prized by gourmet Italians, others are highly poisonous – avoid handling them and visit the local restaurants if you want to taste the best.

WILDLIFE

The hills and mountains and wooded valleys of Umbria are crawling with wildlife. Plentiful wild boar leave telltale hoof prints in the mud but the animals themselves are an extremely rare sight. The young ones, shaped like a rugby ball and coloured like a cappuccino with creamy stripes, sometimes venture out alone, while adult specimens may show their snouts close to villages at dusk. Spectacular but timid crested porcupine carelessly drop their dark brown and cream quills on paths; they were considered a great banquet delicacy by the ancient Romans who brought them to Italy from north Africa. As suggested by road signs warning of their presence, both roe and red deer are common and may well be seen in early morning or towards the close of day, much to the delight of wolves which are gradually returning to Umbria amid controversy.

Snakes are not unusual but the only dangerous species for humans is the viper, recognisable for its silvery diamond markings and easily distinguished from the fast-moving but harmless black colubrid. Very timid, the cold-blooded viper will usually slither away in great haste when approached, often from a path where they have been sunning themselves.

Birds of prey such as kites, kestrel and hawks may also be seen circling overhead, keeping high above the ubiquitous huge grey-black hooded crows that inevitably attempt to chase them off. Open moorland and fields are home to colourful pheasants, who give themselves away with a guttural coughing croak. European jays are a familiar sight, their bright metallic blue plumage glinting in the trees. Woodlands are also home to cuckoos and cooing wood pigeons.

Grassland is often alive with twittering skylarks, alarmed by the presence of humans and intent on launching full-scale alarms. In late spring the hill towns and villages become home to clouds of screeching black swifts who make their home under roof tiles, as well as quieter swallows that build straw and mud nests in overhanging eaves.

GETTING THERE

Several international airports can be used to reach Umbria. The most convenient is Perugia (www.airport. umbria.it). On the Adriatic coast are Ancona (www.aeroportomarche.it) and Pescara (www.abruzzoairport. com). Pisa on the opposite Tyrrhenian

Coast is also an option (www.pisa-airport.com). All have ongoing public transport connections. Both of Rome's airports – Fiumicino (www.adr.it/fiumicino) and Ciampino (www.adr.it/ciampino) – are handy with bus and train links to Umbria. Long-distance coaches (www.sulga.eu) connect Fiumicino with Todi, Perugia and Assisi.

LOCAL TRANSPORT

Excellent centralised network Umbria Mobilità (www.umbriamobilita.it) is the umbrella company for all the public transport you could possibly imagine across the width and breadth of Umbria, from buses and trains to ferries on Lago Trasimeno. Tickets are reasonably priced, and timetables are available on the website. Many of the walks in this guide can be accessed using public transport but be aware that some small villages have no service on Sundays. Several walks do need private transport but hotels will always help arrange for a lift or contact the local taxi for guests who do not have a car.

Bus tickets should be purchased before a journey, either at the bus station or newsstands or tobacconists displaying the appropriate logo; they then need to be stamped on board. However, the drivers do sell tickets on board for a small surcharge.

As far as trains go, buy your ticket at the station. Should the *biglietteria* (ticket office) be closed or the station unstaffed, use the automatic machine. Remember to stamp your ticket before boarding the train. Two rail companies operate in Umbria. Trenitalia (www.trenitalia.com, tel 892021) covers the mainline routes Rome–Florence (Roma–Firenze) and Orte–Foligno–Perugia–Terontola, whereas FCU (see Umbria Mobilità above) does the Terni–Perugia–Sansepolcro lines. The two systems intersect at the Perugia San Giovanni railway station.

Ferry tickets for Lago Trasimeno are sold at landing stages. See the glossary in Appendix B for useful phrases when buying tickets.

INFORMATION

The Italian State Tourist Board (www.enit.it) has offices all over the world and can provide travellers with general information.

Tons of details about accommodation, transport and much else can be got at local tourist information offices, nearly all covered by the website www.umbriatourism.it. Others are given in Appendix C.

WHEN TO GO

'All year round' is the answer for Umbria, although the best times to visit are undoubtedly spring and autumn. As the memory of winter fades, nature comes out of hibernation, leaves unfurl and buds explode overnight, and the hillsides get greener day by day. From March

Low cloud on Monte Cucco

through to early June the weather can be divine for walking – typically long spells of clear conditions with cool mornings and evenings but warm days, prior to the intense heat which can set in from late June through to August. However the summer period can also be beautiful, if busier, and you can head up to the hills and mountains, always the perfect cool retreat if conditions becomes oppressive in the valleys and towns. Autumn (September to October) can bring both clear visibility and crisp air as well as misty conditions, which make for atmospheric photography. During the midwinter months, high mountain districts such as Monte Cucco and the Sibillini will be snowbound – in theory from December to March but there are unpredictable variations year by year.

A slight discouragement to visiting in autumn and winter concerns hunting (*caccia* in Italian): wild boar hunts for example are organised with large groups of dogs and armed participants, so walkers should avoid areas where one is in progress – enquire locally. Generally speaking the season runs through the winter months but hunting is not allowed every day.

ACCOMMODATION

A choice of mostly mid-range hotels and B&Bs handy for the walks is given in Appendix C. Included are cosy family-run places, comfortable hotels in historic palaces, rustic refuges in the mountains, converted monasteries, and simple B&Bs in tiny villages. Prices may vary with the time of year, so check on the websites. Most accept

There are hotels in the very centre of Cascia

internet reservations, and some accept credit cards (check when booking). *Mezza pensione* (half board) is sometimes an option; with breakfast, three-course dinner and the room, it is usually a good deal. For a much greater choice, including self-catering houses, *agriturismo* (farm stays) and camping options, contact the relevant Tourist Offices listed in Appendix C.

You don't usually need to book a long way ahead with the exception of the Italian public holidays: 1 January (New Year), 6 January (Epiphany), Easter Sunday and Monday, 25 April (Liberation Day), 1 May (Labour Day), 2 June (Republic Day), 15 August (Ferragosto), 1 November (All Saints), 8 December (Immaculate Conception), 25–26 December (Christmas and Boxing Day). Weekends are naturally busier too, especially in the 'art towns' such as Assisi, Gubbio, Perugia and Spoleto. Castelluccio is in great demand in early June for the Fiorita, so book ahead for that period.

CULINARY DELIGHTS

Eating and drinking are essential and highly memorable aspects of a holiday in Umbria. It's safe to say that it's impossible to get a bad meal in this Italian region. Good guidelines to follow are: eat local, enquire about seasonal specialities, and, above all, be adventurous. *Che cosa avete oggi?* means 'What's on today?'

Roughly speaking an Italian lunch or dinner menu is divided into five sections: *antipasto* (entrée) followed by *primo* (first course), *secondo* (second course), then *contorno* (vegetables) and *dolce* (dessert).

Olives ripening

Antipasto is mostly cold meats, cheeses or *bruschetta* (toasted bread pieces drizzled with local olive oil or topped with chopped tomatoes or paté). A *primo* is generally pasta which comes in amazing shapes and sizes. For instance *pici*, *umbrichelli* or *strangozzi* are homemade and a bit like spaghetti, whereas *tagliatelle* and *papardelle* are ribbon-like pasta usually coloured yellow with egg yolk. They are served with a vast choice of delicious regional and seasonal sauces including *funghi* (mushrooms), *ragù* (meat sauce) and *arrabbiata* (tomato and chilli). One special topping is the prized black *tartufo* (truffle), a nondescript lumpy tuber that releases an unmistakable perfume when grated or sliced. Ravioli are pasta pockets with luscious fillings such as ricotta and *spinaci* (spinach).

Pulses are widespread, mostly in soups. These include the tiny nutty, sweet *lenticchie* (lentils) that flourish around Castelluccio di Norcia and are justifiably famed all over Italy. Then orangey-yellow *cicerchie* akin to large split peas, known in English as chicklings or grass peas. Fava beans are served fresh or tossed with pasta. *Farro*, a type of spelt, is an ancient cereal used in pasta and breads. Widespread in Roman times, it is considered the cereal par excellence and it gave its name to farina/flour/farinaceous.

Second course is dominated by meat dishes which range from tender cutlets of *agnello* (lamb) often served grilled *scottadito* ('finger scorching'), *cinghiale* (boar) best when stewed, *maiale* (pork), *manzo* (beef) or *vitello* (veal). *Oca* (goose) is common,

'Norcineria' products on sale in Norcia

usually roasted as a mid-August festive offering. Pigeon may be on the menu as *palomba alla leccarda*, with black olives. Another curiosity are *lumache* (snails) served with garlic and parsley. While seafood is understandably uncommon in Umbria, fresh *trota* (trout) is always a good bet (from a river fish farm, *allevamento*) especially if it comes as de-boned fillets. Vegetarians can always request a *frittata* (omelette).

When it is time for vegetables look out for *cicoria* (wild chicory) with a bitter tang and tossed with garlic and chilli, or sweeter *spinaci* with butter. Although not as interesting, fresh *insalata* (salad) is nearly always on offer.

A fitting sweet conclusion to any meal are *tozzetti* or *cantucci*, dry almond biscuits that are matched perfectly with *vin santo*, an amber-coloured dessert wine. Then there's *panna cotta*, a blancmange look-alike served for instance with *frutti di bosco* (berries).

Picnic supplies will usually be *panino con formaggio/prosciutto* – a bread roll with cheese/ham or a flavoursome cold meat such as salami or garlicky *finocchiona* studded with fennel seeds. And do look out for the open-sided vans that do rolls with warm luscious *porchetta* (roast pork), carved up as you wait. Cheese comes in an infinite array of tastes as each valley has its own specialities. Pecorino or sheep cheese is the most common, starting with the soft, fresher varieties through to the more mature, drier versions with a strong tangy bite to them. To infuse special flavour during ripening a cheese may be wrapped in *vinaccia*, the grape skins left after pressing, or even walnut leaves.

Bread (*pane*) in Umbria comes as plain unsalted loaves, roughly sliced and intended to accompany tasty food and not interfere with it. Bakeries often do slabs of oven-fresh pizza or *focaccia*, a mouth-watering variant for picnic lunches. *Crescia* or *torta al testo* is a rare treat these days; a large disc of minimally-leavened bread cooked in the ashes for a delicate scent.

Breakfast tends to be coffee or tea accompanied by cakes, bread, butter and jam. Mid- to upper-range hotels may provide yoghurt, fruit and cereals.

As far as wines go, the Orvieto district produces a crisp dry white, while recommendable white Grechetto hails from the Colli Martani near Todi. The red list is topped by Rosso di Montefalco, Torgiano Rosso Riserva and the stronger Sagrantino.

Unless you have a special penchant for mineral water, it is perfectly acceptable to request *acqua da rubinetto* (tap water) with meals, a small but significant contribution to minimising environmental pollution through unnecessary freight.

WHAT TO TAKE

- Sun protection – a hat, high factor cream and sunglasses
- Lightweight bottle for drinking water
- A small day pack – shoulder and hand-held bags are not a good

Walking through heavenly yellow broom

idea as it is safer to have hands and arms free while walking

- Lightweight trekking boots or a sturdy pair of trainers with good grip and thick soles to protect your feet from loose stones
- Trekking poles for the mountainous routes
- Rainproof gear including a lightweight jacket, rucksack cover and over trousers
- T-shirts and shorts during spring and summer, layered with a light sweater or shirt for cooler conditions. Autumn and winter visitors should pack warmer clothes – long trousers, fleece or pullover, hat and gloves.
- First aid kit
- Whistle, headlamp or torch (with new batteries) for attracting help in an emergency. It is not a good idea to rely on your mobile phone as there is often no signal in outlying places. Note, a torch/headlamp is essential for the tunnels in Walk 30.
- A compass for following maps and identifying landmarks
- Camera, battery recharger and adapter
- Snack food such as muesli bars or biscuits to tide you over if a walk becomes longer than planned

MAPS

Sketch maps are provided alongside each walk in this guidebook. Key landmarks and as much useful detail as possible have been crammed in, dictated by limits of space and graphics. In many cases these maps, along with the detailed route description, are sufficient for the walk. However, it is always a good idea to get hold of the larger commercial maps for many reasons: they put places in a wider context, help you identify points of interest, enable you to plot your own routes and, last but definitely not least, are an essential tool for orientation if you lose your way. Almost all of Umbria is covered by *carta dei sentieri* (walking maps). Relevant maps are listed below with their title, scale, publisher and the walks they cover – although a handful of routes in this guide are not covered by a printed map. Many are available free of charge at tourist offices while others can be purchased locally or online from Florence-based www.stella-alpina.com, as well as bookshops and outdoor specialists overseas.

- Alto Tevere Umbro, Fogli Umbertide e Gubbio 1:40,000 Monte Merli Editrice (Walks 2, 3)
- Alto Tevere Umbro, Fogli Città di Castello e Cagli 1:40,000 Monte Merli Editrice (Walk 1)
- Camminare in Umbria, Trasimeno-Medio Tevere 1:50,000 Istituto Geografico Adriatico (Walks 4, 9, 10, 13, 14, 15, 24, 27)
- Gubbio Carta dei Sentieri 1:25,000 Club Alpino Italiano Sezione di Gubbio (Walks 5, 6)

- Monti di Spoleto e della Media Valnerina 1:25,000 SER (Walks 28, 29, 30, 31, 32)
- Monti Sibillini 1:25,000 SER (Walks 35, 36, 37, 38, 39, 40)
- Monti Sibillini Cascia-Norcia sheet 666 1:50,000 Kompass (Walks 34, 37, 38, 39, 40)
- Orvietano e Trasimeno 1:50,000 Istituto Geografico Adriatico (Walk 18)
- Parco del Lago Trasimeno e Zone Limitrofe 1:25,000 Monte Merli Editrice (Walks 9, 10, 11, 12, 14)
- Parco del Monte Cucco 1:25,000 Monte Meru Editrice (Walks 7, 8)
- Parco del Monte Subasio 1:25,000 Monte Merli Editrice (Walks 25, 26)
- Parco Fluviale del Tevere 1:25,000 Monte Merli Editrice (Walks 19, 20, 21, 22)

DOS AND DON'TS

- Don't set out late on walks even if they are short. Always have extra time up your sleeve to allow for detours and wrong turns.
- Tell your hotel where you will be walking, as a safety precaution
- Find time to get in decent shape before setting out on your holiday, as it will maximise your enjoyment. You will appreciate the scenery better if you're not exhausted, and healthy walkers will react better in an emergency.
- Don't be overly ambitious; choose itineraries suited to your capacity. Read the walk description before setting out.
- Stick with your companions and do not lose sight of them. Remember that you will only go as fast as your slowest member.

The last leg to Monte Patino (Walk 37)

- Route conditions can change, so while walking if you have reasonable doubts about the way to go, never hesitate to turn back and retrace your steps rather than risk getting lost. Better safe than sorry.
- Avoid walking in brand new footwear as it could cause blisters; by the same token, leave those worn-out shoes at home in case they prove unsafe on slippery terrain
- If possible check the weather forecast locally and do not start out, even on a short route, if storms are forecast. Paths can get slippery and mountainsides are prone to rockfalls in storms.
- Carry weatherproof gear at all times, along with food and plenty of drinking water
- In electrical storms, do not shelter under trees or rock overhangs, and keep away from metallic fixtures
- Do not rely on your mobile phone as there may not be any signal
- Carry any rubbish away with you. Even organic waste such as apple cores is best not left lying around as it can upset the diet of animals and birds and spoil things for other visitors.
- Close all stock gates behind you promptly and securely
- Be considerate when making a toilet stop and do not leave unsightly paper lying around. Remember that abandoned huts and rock overhangs could serve as life-saving shelter for someone else.
- English is not widely spoken so make an effort to learn basic greetings: *buongiorno* (good morning), *buona sera* (good evening), *arrivederci* (goodbye) and *grazie* (thank you). See Appendix B for more Italian terms.
- Don't leave your common sense at home

EMERGENCIES

For medical matters, EU residents need a European Health Insurance Card (EHIC). Holders are entitled to free or subsidised emergency treatment in Italy, which has an excellent national health service. Australia has a similar reciprocal agreement – see www.medicareaustralia.gov.au. UK residents should check arrangements post-Brexit. In addition travel insurance to cover a walking holiday is also strongly recommended as costs for rescue and repatriation can be hefty.

The following services may be of help should problems arise. Remember that calls made from a public phone require a coin or pre-paid card to be inserted, although no charge is made for emergency numbers.

- Polizia (police) tel 113
- Tel 118 for health-related urgencies including ambulance (*ambulanza*) and mountain rescue (*soccorso alpino*)

- 'Help!' in Italian is *'Aiuto!'*, pronounced 'eye-you-tow'. *'Pericolo'* is 'danger'.
- To report forest fires tel 1515

USING THIS GUIDE

Each of the 40 walks has been designed to fit into a single day; the majority are circuits with a return to the start point. In addition several wonderful traverses have been included (Walks 18, 22, 27, 30, 31, 33, 36), the return to the start point always possible by public transport.

Many but by no means all routes are waymarked. The majority have the red/white painted stripes of the

Italian Alpine Club (CAI) together with an identifying number. These can be found along the way on prominent stones, trees, walls and rockfaces; small heaps of stone known as cairns are also handy markers. Other routes have local identification as explained in individual walk prefaces. The Sibillini National Park for instance has its own system of lettering and numbering on signs. Where there are no markings, the walk description needs to be followed especially carefully.

Each walk description has an information box containing the following essential data:

Distance Given in kilometres (1km = 0.62 mile).

Clockwise from top left: waymark near Titignano; waymarking on Monte Arale; a CAI marker (this one means you need to turn a corner, it's not an arrow going forwards)

Ascent and descent This is important information, as height gain and loss are an indication of effort required and needs to be taken into account alongside difficulty and distance when planning the day. Generally speaking, a walker of average fitness will cover 300m in ascent in one hour.

Difficulty Each walk has been classified by grade, although adverse weather conditions will make any route more arduous.

- *Grade 1* – an easy route on clear tracks and paths, suitable for beginners (this corresponds approximately to the Italian Alpine Club CAI grade T = *turistico*)
- *Grade 2* – paths across hill and mountain terrain, with lots of ups and downs; a reasonable level of fitness is preferable (this corresponds approximately to CAI grade E = *escursionistico*)
- *Grade 3* – strenuous, and entailing some exposed stretches and possibly prolonged ascent; experience and extra care are recommended (this corresponds approximately to CAI grade EE = *escursionistico esperto*)

Walking time This does not include time out for pauses, picnics, views, photos or nature stops, so as a general rule double the walk times given when planning your day. Every single walker goes at a different pace and makes an unpredictable number of stops along the way, so the 'skeleton' times given are a guide. Times given during the descriptions are partial (as opposed to cumulative).

'Path' is used to mean a narrow pedestrian-only way, 'track' and 'lane' are unsurfaced but vehicle-width, while 'road' is sealed and open to traffic unless specified otherwise. 'SS' means *strada statale*, a main road, whereas 'SP' is *strada provinciale*, minor and usually quieter. Compass bearings are abbreviated (N, S, NNW and so on). Reference landmarks and places encountered en route are in bold type, with their altitude in metres above sea level given as 'm' (100m = 328ft).

Visitors wishing to do more – and the choice is huge – can check the websites listed in Appendix C, in addition to those of local CAI branches. Any number of routes can be concocted with the aid of a good map. A warning: some exist only on paper so before embarking on a walk not described in this guidebook, enquire locally as to the current state of the route.

1 ALTA VAL TIBERINA, GUBBIO AND MONTE CUCCO

INTRODUCTION

A view of medieval Montone (Walk 2)

Before you lies a broad, extended plain bounded by a range of mountains, whose summits are covered with tall and ancient woods, stocked with all kinds of game. At their foot the eye runs along one unbroken stretch of vineyards and crops.

Pliny the Younger (1st century AD) was enthusing about the Alta Val Tiberina (which translates as the Upper Tiber Valley). Accounting for the northern-most branch of Umbria squeezed in between Tuscany and Marche, it ventures to the edge of the wild Apennines chain. Woodland and farming characterise this down-to-earth district and good bases for visitors include Città di Castello (Walk 1) and Umbertide,

both served by the FCU minor branch railway that runs between Perugia and Sansepolcro. A short bus trip from Umbertide is delightful hillside Montone (Walks 2 and 3).

Of the mountains mentioned by the Roman geographer framing the broad valley, prominent elongated Monte Tezio, visited in Walk 4, stands out as a landmark on the western flanks. Over the centuries much of the woods have been cleared for pasture, a great boon for walkers who can enjoy marvellous wide-ranging views.

Heading northeast, the rolling hills are run through by countless rivers and streams. One is Torrente Saonda that traverses an agricultural plain dominated by fascinating and welcoming walled Renaissance Gubbio with tons of interest for culture vultures and walkers alike. The town grew up at the base of Monte Ingino, which boasts an historic open-sided lift used to access Walk 6. Neighbouring Monte Foce is visited in Walk 5. Gubbio is well served by a multitude of buses including links with Umbertide as well as the railway at Fossato di Vico.

Continuing inland, Valle del Chiascio is revealed. It becomes immediately obvious that the rural river valley is overshadowed by immense Monte Cucco, which straddles the northeastern edge of Umbria and its boundary with Marche. The bareness of Monte Cucco's western slopes can be attributed to the ancient Romans who stripped it of trees to feed the bathhouse furnaces in the capital. Grazing sheep and cows have contributed, and account for the curious parallel ruts. In stark contrast are the luxuriant beech woods cloaking the eastern slopes, slinking in and out of gullies and chasms cut deep by running streams. Buses are limited to the main valley so a car is essential here. From Sigillo a road climbs 10km, providing access for Rifugio Valletta and Walk 7, as well as atmospheric wooded Val di Ranco (Walk 8) where Albergo Monte Cucco nestles. A regional park, it is popular with hang gliders, walkers and spelunkers attracted to the limestone caves.

The Chiascio River meanders southwards, finally making up its mind to join the Tiber's flow in the proximity of wonderful Perugia, regional capital, nerve centre and transport hub for the Umbria region. Layered over ancient Etruscan foundations, the superb city is well worth a multi-day visit; however, it is rather too spread out to be a useful base for walks as you spend too much time getting out of and back into the place.

Photogenic Castello del Procoio (Walk 4)

WALK 1
Monte Santa Maria Tiberina

Start/Finish	Palazzetto, Monte Santa Maria Tiberina
Distance	10km
Ascent/Descent	200m/200m
Difficulty	Grade 1–2
Walking time	3hr
Maps	Alto Tevere Umbro, Fogli Città di Castello e Cagli 1:40,000 Monte Merli Editrice
Refreshments	In Monte Santa Maria Tiberina, there is a tiny grocery shop and café alongside Ristorante Oscari and its panoramic terrace.
Public transport	Monte Santa Maria Tiberina is linked to Città di Castello by a weekday bus.
Access	The Palazzetto crossroads can be found on the western approach to Monte Santa Maria Tiberina, 1km from the town centre.

Beautiful Monte Santa Maria Tiberina is a tranquil hill town close to where Umbria meets Tuscany in the Upper Tiber Valley. Perched on a mountainous conifer-clad knoll, the settlement is dominated by a splendid rambling grey stone palazzo-cum-castle in 17th-century style. In the winter months when the winds are piercingly chilly, the population shrinks to 16 – the faithful restaurateur included – and they occasionally get snowed in. However, during summer when the plains cities are sweltering, Monte Santa Maria Tiberina guarantees cooling breezes – and that's when foreign and Italian property owners return, bringing life.

This pleasant ring walk (Anello n.10) starts a short distance below the town walls and follows a series of lanes and unmade roads. It wanders through woodland and open fields, and opportunities abound for appreciating the lovely hilly rural ambience. Red/white waymarking is mostly clear and frequent except for a couple of spots on the return leg, when extra care is needed at forks.

From **Palazzetto** (617m) and the mapboard showing the itinerary, take quiet country road Via San Martino SW

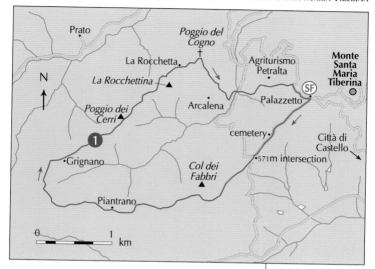

along a ridge through a rural area. It descends past the cemetery to an **intersection** (571m), continuing straight ahead and unsurfaced between open fields with views across rolling countryside dotted with farms. There are gentle ups and downs as woodland alternates with open moorland colonised by scented broom, orchids and pheasants. The way bears gradually W past **Col dei Fabbri** to touch on the abandoned 11th-century hamlet of **Piantrano** (637m). An uphill stretch leads to a power pole where you ignore the signed fork left (n.156) and continue on a short way towards Poggio dei Contadini to the turn-off right for n.153a (1hr).

Go N at first on a sometimes muddy track through masses of broom – keep right at the next fork as marked by red/white on a tree – and alongside a small pine plantation soon in descent NE on a rougher lane. The isolated houses of **Grignano** (676m) are touched on and you get nice views to the hamlet of Prato well below. Further downhill past masses of tree heather and **Poggio dei Cerri** is a saddle where the way veers left to avoid the knoll **La**

31

Soon after Poggio del Cogno, the village comes into sight

If you enter the hamlet of Arcalena, you've missed the turn-off.

Rocchettina, dropping steeply to the cluster of houses **La Rocchetta** (545m). Continue NE on the lane – n.153 now – keeping left on the lower lane at derelict houses soon encountered. At the saddle **Poggio del Cogno** (538m, 1hr) and an old wooden cross, Monte Santa Maria Tiberina comes into sight, impressive on its remarkable perch.

Go right here (still n.153), and after about 5min, as the lane curves right, leave it for a faint track left (red/white marking on tree). ◄ This drops SE through woodland, bearing right past a field, then down and over a stream, Fosso Erchi (640m). Cross straight over an unmade road and up the other side, following the red/white markings through woodland. Further up, as you reach farm buildings, fork right through the property and up through a wire gate to join a decent lane. Here, at a sign for **Agriturismo Petralta** go right uphill to the tarmac – fork right again and in a matter of minutes you will be back at **Palazzetto** (617m, 1hr).

WALK 2
Monte Falcone

Start/Finish	Piazza Fortebraccio, Montone
Distance	8.2km
Ascent/Descent	315m/315m
Difficulty	Grade 2
Walking time	2hr 15min
Maps	Alto Tevere Umbro, Fogli Umbertide e Gubbio 1:40,000 Monte Merli Editrice
Refreshments	Montone has a grocery shop, café and restaurants.
Public transport	Occasional weekday buses link the village with Umbertide.
Access	Piazza Fortebraccio is the central square in the village of Montone. Park outside the walls.

Beginning in utterly medieval Montone in the Upper Tiber Valley, this wonderful loop climbs up and down ridges through the rolling farming district. For the most part it follows easy lanes, but be aware that the central section takes steep paths first down then up abrupt hillsides, possibly with overgrown tracts. Overall, waymarking is clear and fairly constant, however, extra care is essential in the woods so as not to lose the way. The first stretch is in common with a longer route, Walk 3.

From **Piazza Fortebraccio** (482m) walk past the Municipio building and under the covered archway bearing a plaque to Polidori, a local boy who fought with Garibaldi. ▶ Outside the walls, turn left to the corner and benches and take the path forking right in descent 'Percorso pedonale Macchia del Negrone'. Steps lead past picnic tables to an abandoned **church and mapboard** on the roadside. Turn right here but soon branch left (N) off the road on a lane with red/white marking and signed n.111. It is not far uphill past a fork for Cardaneto to where the path shortcuts through open woodland where orchids bloom. The lane is resumed further up for a lovely stretch amid cultivated fields and vistas over the Upper Tiber Valley towards Città di Castello as well as back to photogenic Montone.

The piazza is named after the 15th-century condottiero Fortebraccio – meaning 'strong arm'!

33

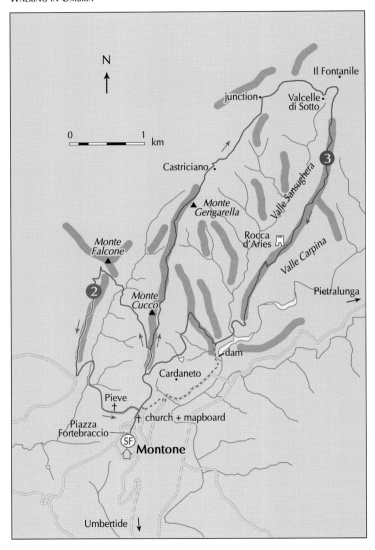

N

0   1 km

Il Fontanile

junction

Valcelle
di Sotto

Castriciano

▲ *Monte
Gengarella*

Valle Sansughera

*Monte
Falcone*
▲

Rocca
d'Aries

3

2

Valle Carpina

*Monte
Cucco*
▲

Pietralunga

dam

Cardaneto

Pieve
✝

+ church + mapboard

Piazza
Fortebraccio

SF

Montone

Umbertide ↓

The walk begins in the village square, Piazza Fortebraccio

At a fork, keep left (NW) on the white gravel lane signed n.111b for Monte Falcone (parting ways with n.111/Walk 3 to Rocca d'Aries). You continue on the midriff of Monte Cucco past cypress trees, looking over rolling rich farmland and a patchwork of yellow and green fields. As the lane reaches a farm, keep to the upper way past sheds to where waymarks point you downhill left. Bear right around a vineyard for the start of a plunge into the woods. Watch your step and be sure to follow the red/white paint stripes on the trees. The path narrows progressively, ending up at the bottom of the valley where a stream needs crossing. This area may be a little overgrown. Markers lead up the other side to a power line and a steep but clearer slog NW to finally emerge at a small olive grove. Keep left up to a lane then right to a signed junction below a house on **Monte Falcone** (539m, 1hr 15min).

The way is more straightforward from now on. Branch left on the wide lane S in gentle descent along a scenic ridge alternating conifers with mixed wood and fields. Soon, as well as the attractive expanse of fields and rows of trees on the plain, the outlook takes in triangular Monte Acuto northwest beyond Montone. About 30 minutes from Monte Falcone as you approach a surfaced road, the marked route n.111 suddenly forks sharp left (NE) down a muddy sheep track and over a stream. Accompanied by poplar trees it resumes the southerly direction parallel to the watercourse before heading uphill along the very edge of a field. It finally emerges on a quiet road amid olive trees and a vineyard, and turns left. Past **Pieve**, an old church and adjoining farm, it joins the Pietralunga road where you go right. The abandoned church and mapboard are soon reached, where you turn right uphill to return to **Montone** (482m, 1hr).

The village comes back into view towards the end of the walk

WALK 3
Rocca d'Aries

Start/Finish	Piazza Fortebraccio, Montone
Distance	15km
Ascent/Descent	550m/550m
Difficulty	Grade 2
Walking time	4hr 15min
Maps	Alto Tevere Umbro, Fogli Umbertide e Gubbio 1:40,000 Monte Merli Editrice (partial coverage)
Refreshments	Montone has groceries, café and restaurants.
Public transport	Occasional weekday buses link the village with Umbertide.
Access	Piazza Fortebraccio is the central square in the village of Montone. Park outside the walls.

This superb albeit lengthy circuit starts out from the beautiful walled village of Montone along a series of wonderfully scenic ridges, woodland and rural landscapes to the landmark castle Rocca d'Aries, also spelt Aria. It corresponds to the local Anello 17 (ring route 17); signposted forks and red/white waymarking are fairly constant although by no means omnipresent so it is important to keep an eye out. The first stretch is in common with Walk 2, a shorter route.

▶ From **Piazza Fortebraccio** (482m) walk past the Municipio building and under covered archways bearing a plaque to Polidori, a local boy who fought with Garibaldi. Outside the walls turn left to the corner and benches for the path forking right in descent 'Percorso pedonale Macchia del Negrone'. Steps lead past picnic tables to an abandoned **church and mapboard** on the roadside. Turn right here to a batch of signposts where you branch left uphill (N) on n.111. It is not far to the fork for Cardaneto (where the return route slots back in) – ignore it for the time being and keep on to where the path shortcuts through light wood bright with wild orchids. The unsurfaced road is resumed further up on a lovely stretch amid cultivated fields with vistas over the Upper Tiber Valley and to photogenic Montone.

For route map see Walk 2.

The walk leaves the village by way of brick archways

Ignore the fork left for Monte Falcone (Walk 2) and continue through pine woods on the eastern flank of **Monte Cucco**. Further on keep eyes peeled for a right-hand branch and an old path that loops parallel to the main ridge, rejoining the unsurfaced road after about 5min. Not far on after that, where the road begins to curve left, n.111 leaves it once more to branch right again for a climb over eroding grey rock layers, enjoying lovely views across wild wooded hills to Rocca d'Aries due east. At a modest cairn, bear left up to the ridge and into the trees where red/white waymarks reappear, pointing you NNE. This soon emerges on flat open **Monte**

Gengarella (604m). A clear lane proceeds to ruined house **Castriciano** (601m, 1hr 15min).

The unsurfaced road is rejoined at this point, and you branch right (NNE) skirting a knoll to stroll between pine trees and Mediterranean vegetation. At a signposted junction (15min) fork right (E) on a path in descent along the edge of a field and down to a track in the company of a trickling stream. A short climb leads across a field and on to the isolated house Valcelle di Sotto (514m), looking over olive groves and wheat fields. Now you follow a gravel lane to two consecutive signposted junctions and the gateway to **Il Fontanile** property, where the lane (n.114 now) heads S. After a short stretch uphill to a saddle comes a right-hand branch (S) along a beautifully panoramic ridge separating **Valle Carpina** and **Valle Sansughera**, and smothered in scented broom. Occupying a commanding position is elegant tower-cum-castle **Rocca d'Aries** (520m, 1hr 20min) looking east-northeast to the rugged Apennines.

Soon the lane is interrupted by a house – easily detoured by a rocky rougher path which swings downhill in wide bends essentially S. It concludes in the valley

Rocca d'Aries is a worthy destination

(318m) near a renovated property. Branch right along the dirt road across a bridge and soon to a junction (45min). A slightly shorter (by 10min) but more straightforward return to Montone is feasible here.

Alternative return to Montone
Stay on the dirt road past the **dam**. Around the corner, tarmac is joined and a bridge over Torrente Carpina passed (without crossing). Continue SW for 0.5km to where n.115 forks right as a path that follows an open metal pipe uphill. This reaches a road where you go right to the batch of signposts and then the abandoned **church and mapboard**, where you need to go left up to **Montone**.

Go right (NW) at the junction along the lane access to a house. Here a less trodden route takes over, crossing a stream in woodland and soon climbing over an eroded rise. Now a faint path continues down to cross a second side stream before touching on a pond. A subsequent steep uphill stretch emerges on a gravel road close to the photogenic hamlet of **Cardaneto**, with a lovely view of Montone backed by mountains. Turn right and you soon rejoin the unsurfaced road followed on the outward stretch. Branch left in descent to the **church** and another left to return to **Montone** (482m, 1hr).

WALK 4
Monte Tezio

Start/Finish	Migiana di Monte Tezio
Distance	12km
Ascent/Descent	550m/550m
Difficulty	Grade 2
Walking time	3hr 30min
Maps	Camminare in Umbria 1:50,000 Trasimeno-Medio Tevere, Istituto Geografico Adriatico
Refreshments	Nothing is available locally or during the walk.
Access	Whichever way you approach the hamlet of Migiana, it means driving along a winding and narrow road, with the final 2km unmade. The shortest route (8km) from Val Tiberina forks off from Ponte Pattoli, which is located about halfway between Perugia and Umbertide. Park by the church in Migiana.

This must-do circuit walk traverses magnificently scenic Monte Tezio, a modest slumbering massif set on the western edge of the Upper Tiber Valley north of Perugia. Its 960m summit and broad adjoining crests are mainly grassland, pasture for the sheep and cows left to graze here in summer. But for walkers the implication is quite different – all-round views over what feels like the whole of Umbria, plus the rugged Apeninnes.

Paths are clear and waymarking good and frequent – follow red/white M22. However, stable weather with good visibility is essential as orientation on the featureless top could be difficult and even dangerous in mist or low cloud. Carry plenty of water, food and sun protection. The walk begins by circling the base of Monte Tezio before tackling the straightforward climb to the broad uppermost crest. Later on, the undemanding descent touches on photogenic Castello di Procoio or Procopio, recently renovated and rebaptised Santa Eurasia.

From **Migiana di Monte Tezio** (529m) take the lane N away from the village and past the **cemetery**. Around the corner is a rambling homestead, then it is NW in gentle descent and past a traffic barrier for the forestry reserve (Azienda Forestale di Somonte). Light woodland

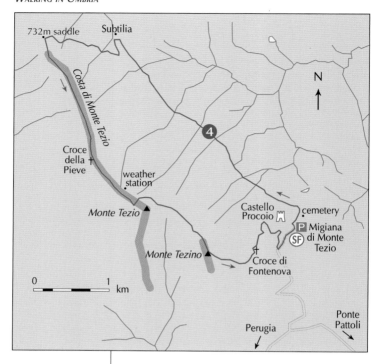

alive with birdsong and bright with cyclamens accounts for these lower eastern flanks of Monte Tezio, while to your right (east) are rolling wooded hills dotted with tiny hamlets. A couple of abandoned farms are encountered along the way. Stick to the waymarked lane as far as the gated property **Subtilia** (aka Casale Pavie), where the outlook north takes in Antognolla, its castle and golf course. Almost immediately after it, leave the lane for the signed path left (520m, 1hr). Well graded it climbs in wide zigzags into beech wood. As the gradient becomes more gentle, you bear NW to emerge on open grassland dotted with juniper shrubs, orchids and alive with skylarks. At a saddle (732m) the horizons enlarge with magnificent

views to neighbouring Monte Acuto as well as Lago
Trasimeno southwest.

Now head left (SSE) up **Costa di Monte Tezio**, the
ever-improving panorama encompassing the rugged
Apennines east, including the Sibillini range, snowcapped well into the spring. A stone hut is passed adjacent a tree-filled karstic depression, which testifies to the
limestone rock here. A series of pink rock slabs lead S to
Croce della Pieve (942m, 1hr 10min), a marvellous lookout where Monte Cetona and triangular Amiata are easily recognisable southwest. Ignore the fork right (Sentiero
3) and stay on the broad windswept crest, soon curving
left in descent past a narrow rock chasm, not far from a
weather station. After another shrub-filled *dolina*, near a
sign for a 'neviere' (old snow store) veer decidedly left
(initially N) on a faint track circling below grassy **Monte
Tezio**. The track quickly becomes clearer and faint red/
white markings on rocks more evident as it heads SE
accompanied by thorny flowering shrubs. Across a saddle it is uphill once more to the antennas on **Monte
Tezino** (920m, 30min), which looks over to the city of
Perugia and the rest of Umbria.

Keep left around the fenced enclosure to follow
the cairns SE down the grassy slopes. ▶ As you reach
the edge of wood, veer left to the iron cross **Croce di**

At your feet is
Migiana and the
landmark Castello di
Procoio, to the east
Assisi stands out on
the lower flanks of
bare-topped Monte
Subasio, which
curiously resembles
a volcano from this
angle.

A scenic picnic can be enjoyed on Monte Tezio

Fontenova (700m) with a bird's-eye vista of the castle and hamlet. Keep left into broom thickets and light woodland on a stony path with overgrown stretches. As it reaches a rough lane, go right to pass the entrance to **Castello di Procoio** and out to the unmade road. By branching left you will soon find yourself back at the church and **Migiana di Monte Tezio** (529m, 50min).

WALK 5
Monte Foce

Start/Finish	Porta Santa Croce, Gubbio
Distance	7km
Ascent/Descent	475m/475m
Difficulty	Grade 2
Walking time	2hr 45min
Maps	Gubbio Carta dei sentieri 1:25,000 Club Alpino Italiano Sezione di Gubbio. City map free from the Tourist Office; its photographic map is also helpful.
Refreshments	Take a picnic from Gubbio.
Access	Porta Santa Croce is Gubbio's northwestern gate. From landmark Piazza Grande in the town centre, take Via dei Consoli W. As it descends, either fork right on the pedestrian-only route along the old walls to a covered footbridge, or keep on down to a bridge then right along Via del Camignano, concluding at the gate. Allow 15 minutes in either case.

This is a very rewarding and varied circular walk setting out directly from beautiful medieval Gubbio, an absolute delight. The destination is neighbouring Monte Foce. After touching on a monastery and making its way through woodland, this walk offers grandiose views to both Gubbio itself and its valley, and, if you are lucky with a cloudless day, over the vast rugged Apennines as well.

The walk route is well marked with red/white paint splashes and n.252. As concerns difficulty it rates average as after Sant'Ambrogio the path narrows for short sections with a little exposure but nothing problematical.

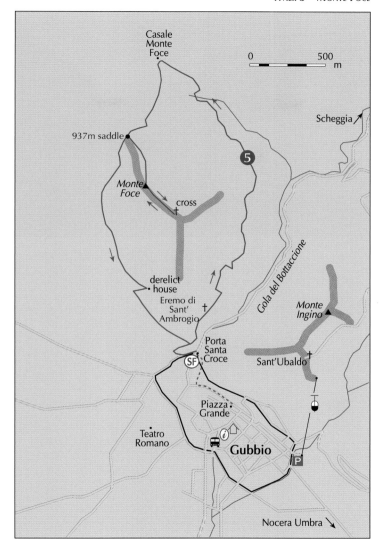

Casale
Monte
Foce

0   500
m

Scheggia

5

937m saddle

*Monte
Foce*
cross

Gola del Bottaccione

derelict
house

*Monte
Ingino*

Eremo di
Sant'
Ambrogio

Porta
Santa
Croce

SF

Sant'Ubaldo

Piazza
Grande

Teatro
Romano

Gubbio

P

Nocera Umbra

The walk begins in lower Gubbio

From Gubbio's **Porta Santa Croce** aka Porta Metauro (510m) in the Quartiere di San Martino, turn left along the main road Via del Fosso outside the town walls. Soon on the right is a forked ramp – take the left branch signed for 'S Ambrogio/n.252'. Not far up the narrow surfaced road branch right again and pass a towering stone wall corner where the return route joins back in. Proceed NNE up steps to the peaceful monastery **Eremo di Sant'Ambrogio** (598m, 15min). Along with lovely views back to Gubbio, here you can enjoy the sight of the medieval aqueduct that snakes its way along the lower slopes of Monte Ingino opposite. Far below stretches the Gola del Bottaccione.

> The sedimentary rock strata of the **Gola del Bottaccione** has been found to contain unusually high concentrations of the naturally occurring metal iridium, key marker of the catastrophic meteorite that is recognised as the primary cause of the extinction of the dinosaurs and plant life.

The path continues to an anti-rockfall barrier where it forks sharp left uphill along wire fencing. Steep zigzags follow through woodland brightened with cyclamens. The gradient finally eases off as the way becomes a lovely traverse N. ▶

As the path narrows, occasional stretches feel a little exposed but as it bears left (NW) into conifer wood the way widens considerably. Ignore turn-offs and continue in gentle ascent to a farm lane. Join it left uphill to a farm **Casale Monte Foce** on a corner (822m, 1hr). With a view both over a quarry and up to the top of Monte Foce, continue climbing on the lane S through fields and pasture above the treeline now, in the company of red/white markings. After a drinking trough for cattle (recycled old bath tubs) the lane bears right up to a **saddle** (937m, 15min).

For the final leg to the mountaintop, branch left (SE) dodging cowpats and grazing livestock and surprising skylarks. Follow the broad ridge to the actual top of **Monte Foce** (983m) for fantastic views, but proceed a little further on to the **iron cross** (975m, 15min) for spectacular bird's-eye views over Gubbio and its valley, not to

As you pass under white cliffs, evidence of an old road is visible underfoot, while aromatic Mediterranean plants and gorgeous broom flourish on sun-blessed corners.

Views down to medieval Gubbio and its monuments

mention most of Umbria and the Apennine chain including Monte Cucco and the Sibillini.

Return to the **saddle** and go left on the stony path SSW across the rutted mountainside and into conifer wood. Clearings afford more views over the patchwork of cultivated fields and soon to Gubbio's landmark Teatro Romano. A steep descent on a loose gravel path lined with aromatic everlasting plants concludes at a **derelict house** (Casa Vena). Fork sharp left here in constant descent SE through mixed wood, finally reaching the stone wall corner encountered near the walk start. Turn right here down the road back to **Porta Santa Croce** (510m, 1hr).

WALK 6

Above Gubbio

Start/Finish	Funivia, Gubbio
Distance	11km
Ascent/Descent	330m/660m
Difficulty	Grade 2
Walking time	3hr
Maps	Carta dei sentieri 1:25,000 Club Alpino Italiano Sezione di Gubbio. The Gubbio Tourist Office free photographic map with paths superimposed is also helpful.
Refreshments	Several café-restaurants are located near the lift arrival on the mountain, and there is Ristorante Parco Coppo at the playground although it closes off-season.
Access	The year-round lift www.funiviagubbio.it is to be found in the upper eastern edge of town. Car parking is free there.

Beginning with the thrilling, wobbly ride from Gubbio in the open-sided cage referred to grandiosely as the 'funivia' (cable car) up the front of Monte Ingino, the walk meanders across wooded rural valleys. Afterwards it descends on a panoramic – although narrow and moderately exposed – path back to town, entering through the original 13th-century walls in a lovely conclusion.

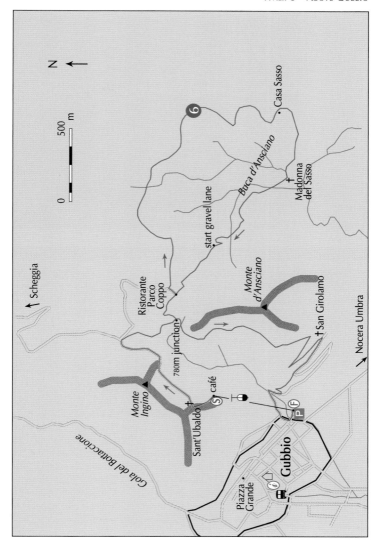

Bird's-eye views over Gubbio from the open-sided lift

SEASONAL HIGHLIGHTS

There are some seasonal highlights to bear in mind in this part of Umbria. In May, Sant'Ubaldo is the destination for a madcap race of teams lugging three huge 'ceri', wooden towers topped by statues of saints, which are lugged up from Piazza Grande by teams in medieval costume.

Come winter, Monte Ingino is transformed into a gigantic Christmas tree – the largest in the world – illuminated by 800 light bulbs and 20km of electric wiring!

After the funivia trip to the café terrace at 827m, follow the signs up steps to nearby **Basilica di Sant'Ubaldo**. Then go right (NE) for half a kilometre on the quiet SP209 road lined with cypresses and conifers. Keep right at the first fork (where the road bears left for Scheggia and Gubbio) and immediately afterwards branch right onto a lane marked red/white n.251B. This quickly leads down to a hollow for an easy-to-miss fork abrupt left (red/white markings) uphill via a narrowish ledge and into conifer wood. A few minutes ahead is the junction for San Girolamo (780m, 30min) where this loop returns later.

For the time being branch left (signed 'n.251/253') around a knoll to a playground and **Ristorante Parco Coppo**. On the left side of the building turn right along the road (n.253), which quickly becomes unsurfaced, passing through mixed wood. Stick to the lane even at the gate bearing the intimidating 'proprietà privata' sign (applicable only to vehicles). Now comes a leisurely stroll in gentle descent entering the **Buca d'Ansciano** valley; take care to follow red/white n.253 at the many turn-offs. At **Casa Sasso** (613m), set beautifully on an outcrop, the lane veers left, curving W downhill to picnic tables near the tiny chapel of **Madonna del Sasso** (578m, 1hr).

> Peek inside this chapel for the **revered old image of Mary**. According to legend, it was painted either by a hunter, grateful he had survived a shot from his own rifle, or a farmer, who scrambled out alive after his oxen and cart slid into a chasm.

Next, just above the building and opposite the picnic area you need to leave the lane for a faint path; it climbs NW over light grey crumbly rock layers and into

The tiny chapel of Madonna del Sasso

51

woodland where red/white marking and n.254 appear soon. It wastes no time in climbing steeply past masses of broom, wild roses and juniper to a field. Keep around its edge to a prominent oak tree where a lane resumes up to buildings that are part of the Parco di Coppo property. A white gravel lane bordered with cypresses leads back up to Ristorante Parco Coppo. Ignore the signed path for 'Gubbio' and instead branch left around the playground as per the outward route. Back at the afore-mentioned junction (780m, 40min), take the direction for San Girolamo – namely left (S). ◄

If desired, limit yourself to the upper loop, turn right here and return to town by way of the funivia.

A lovely level path cuts along **Monte d'Ansciano** in and out of the wood, with narrow stretches that tend on exposed at times. Gorgeous views to Gubbio and the plain beyond can naturally be expected. Wider stony lane n.261 is eventually joined – and here you go right alongside wire netting in descent to **San Girolamo** (651m, 30min), a convent for closeted Clarissa nuns. Take the quiet surfaced road Via San Girolamo past the line-up of artistic stations of the cross, continuing straight ahead (NW) on the marked shortcut at the first bend. The road is resumed under the funivia and through the ancient town walls. Walk down the street and under covered arches until you come to the fork left across a footbridge leading to the car park at the **Gubbio** funivia once more (532m, 20min).

The descent path is quite narrow

52

WALK 7
Monte Cucco

Start/Finish	Decollo Sud car park
Distance	6.2km
Ascent/Descent	370m/370m
Difficulty	Grade 2–3
Walking time	2hr 30min
Maps	Parco del Monte Cucco 1:25,000 Monte Meru Editrice
Refreshments	Rifugio Valletta has a café-restaurant, otherwise take a picnic from Sigillo.
Access	Decollo Sud, the take-off point for para and hang gliders, is also known as Pian di Monte. It is located a short distance from Rifugio Valletta, where the road from Sigillo terminates.

From the word go this must-do walk to a modest peak in the regional park is superbly panoramic. It circles the upper reaches of Monte Cucco before taking in the actual summit, so the 360° outlook encompasses the vast extension of Umbria. To the east you look over the plains and towns of Le Marche and if you're lucky with little cloud cover, you will see all the way to the Adriatic coast as well! Skylarks are everywhere, while birds of prey circle overhead. In the early summer months the grassy slopes are a carpet of crocus and squill alongside an array of succulents.

However be aware that Monte Cucco belongs to the rugged central Apennine range, and as such is subject to the winds that typically blow in from the west and the Tyrrhenian Sea, buffeting against the mountainous ridges before dropping east down to the Adriatic. It is inadvisable to embark on this walk in high winds or low cloud as you can easily become disoriented, lose your way on the steep mountainsides. Even in good conditions the walk rates as fairly difficult in view of the narrow and moderately exposed stretches of path.

From **Decollo Sud** (1197m) take the clear track that strikes out across the grassy slopes, curving N in ascent as a rough stony lane n.2/15. Bearing left, it reaches the wooden **guides' cabin** (Rifugio Valcella) used for visits to the nearby cave (see Appendix C). Fork left here up to the

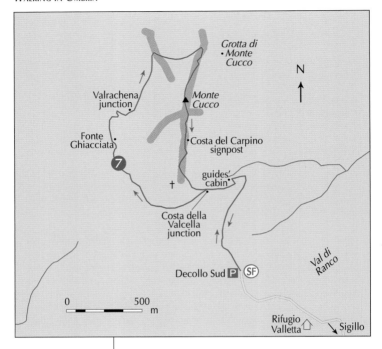

signed junction on **Costa della Valcella** (1335m, 40min). Here branch left again on n.15 for a superbly panoramic path that cuts the steep grassed western flanks of Monte Cucco. Well below, the town of Sigillo can be seen in upper Valle del Chiascio with Costacciaro further around.

At **Fonte Ghiacciata** and its water troughs the terrain becomes stonier and pitted with tiny fossils. A short climb on a faint path leads to where n.2 is encountered. Go right and over a saddle to the signed junction of **Valrachena** (1423m, 30min). Keep ahead (still on n.2) in ascent through young beech wood alongside a black pipe. Where the trees are left behind the views open up fantastically north and northeast. At a corner keep right on n.2 (the other unnumbered path leads to a cave exit)

as the way narrows and traverses steeper grassy slopes. At the ensuing fork turn right on n.14 for the stiff leg to the crest and tiny wood cross marking the actual top of **Monte Cucco** (1566m, 30min). Phew! What a view!

Admiring the Valle del Chiascio

Duly rested, follow the cairns and red/white rock markings along the ridge. ▶ Head for the **signpost** ('Costa del Carpino', 1511m) to look down to the Decollo Sud area and beyond over the rugged Apennine chain. The faint path heads essentially S from here on – do not be tempted by the large iron cross to the right – to reach the Costa della Valcella junction (1335m, 25min) encountered on the way up. Then retrace your steps to the Decollo Sud car park (1197m, 25min).

Take great care here not to venture over the precipitous edges!

55

WALK 8
Val di Rio Freddo

Start/Finish	Albergo Monte Cucco
Distance	8.5km
Ascent/Descent	340m/340m
Difficulty	Grade 1–2
Walking time	3hr 20min
Maps	Parco del Monte Cucco 1:25,000 Monte Meru Editrice
Refreshments	Pian delle Macinare has a café-restaurant that is open through summer and most weekends; otherwise buy a picnic at Albergo Monte Cucco.
Access	Albergo Monte Cucco is located in Val di Ranco, on a turn-off towards the end of the road from Sigillo. 'Villaggio Turistico' on signs refers to the cluster of holiday homes in Val di Ranco.

This lovely walk explores the cascading streams and enchanting beechwood in Val di Rio Freddo on the eastern flanks of Monte Cucco, where exemplars in the Madre dei Faggi wood are as old as 400 years. It is a lovely introductory wander to the park areas with plenty of variety.

Be aware that Monte Cucco is subject to mist, so expect to encounter slippery conditions on the rock slabs alongside the watercourses – watch your step. Also, after heavy rain the streams will be fuller, so wear waterproof non-slip boots.

A few metres back up the road leading to **Albergo Monte Cucco** (1058m) is a small chapel where you need to take the lane Viale San Pietro (n.10bis) heading N. Keep left at the first fork and continue past the holiday houses in woodland. The way soon becomes a path in descent through bushy vegetation on **Monte Culumeo**. You look over to Monte Lo Spicchio, its flanks patterned with intersecting ruts left by decades of grazing livestock. After a stretch E, at the floor of **Valle San Pietro** turn sharp left following the stream, which soon descends in a series of lovely cascades over rock slabs in shady beech wood.

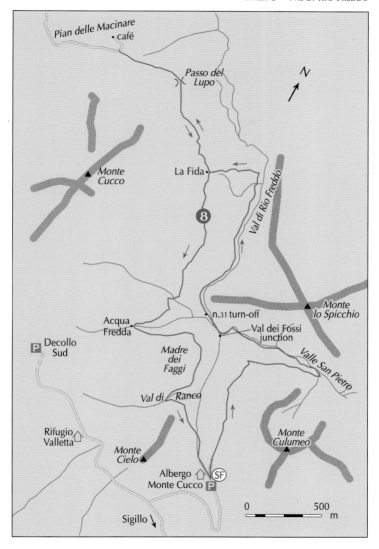

Following a cascading stream in Valle San Pietro

Keep an eye out for the red/white waymarks as the path criss-crosses the watercourse making its way W. At the **Val dei Fossi junction** (957m, 40min) keep straight ahead on n.3, NW at first. A short way along, ignore the turn-off for n.31 and continue mostly N on another delightful stretch of stream fords and woodland in **Val di Rio Freddo**. At a grassy clearing with wild rose bushes and a good view of Monte Cucco and the summit up to your left, hunt around for the sign and branch left on n.17. A short climb brings you to a broader path at **La Fida** (1001m, 40min).

Now it is right (NW) on n.1 uphill past a fork for Voragine Boccanera (for expert cavers) and steeply at times on to a cliff corner and the belvedere **Passo del Lupo** ('wolf's pass', 1155m) with its lovely outlook northeast across hills and fields. A short way WSW brings you to the beautiful grassy clearing, or 'dolina', of **Pian delle Macinare** (1134m, 30min). ◄ It is ringed with beech wood and, judging from the widespread digging and scratching marks, is popular with wild boar. It is also a great favourite with two-legged visitors who come up to picnic.

A dolina is a shallow depression in limestone caused by water erosion.

Retrace your steps on n.1 to La Fida junction (1001m, 20min) and continue on the wide path SSE to the spring/drinking fountain **Acqua Fredda** (1015m) and picnic area. Here a broad lane is joined for the stroll through the wondrous mossy ancient beech wood known as **Madre dei Faggi**. The winding way leads back to where you started at **Albergo Monte Cucco** (1058m, 1hr 10min).

2 LAGO TRASIMENO AND ENVIRONS

Old street in Passignano (Walk 10)

INTRODUCTION

The ferry nears Isola Polvese (Walk 12)

A short train trip to the west of the regional capital Perugia, Lago Trasimeno comes as quite a surprise in hilly Umbria. As Italy's fourth largest lake it has a lot going for it. According to legend, Trasimeno was a handsome Etruscan prince hopelessly enamoured of a lake nymph who lured him to an island; alas he drowned en route and on balmy summer evenings, her laments are carried over the water by the breeze. More experienced swimmers may enjoy a dip at one of the modest beaches – between March and October water temperature averages 21°C. Passing by in the 1870s, the American writer Henry James commented: 'Between Perugia and Cortona lies the large weedy waste of Lake Thrasymene, turned into a witching word for ever by Hannibal's recorded victory over Rome.' And what a battle that was! See Walk 9 to find out what the great Carthaginian general got up to.

Passignano on the north shore is an excellent base as it has train, bus and ferry connections, accommodation as well as an intact medieval heart. Walk 10 begins there. A promontory on the opposite shore is the enviable location of lovely Castiglione del Lago, also served by buses and ferries. The lake's two attractive islands are Isola Maggiore (Walk 11) with eateries and a small hotel, while in

Lago Trasimeno (Walk 9)

the south is the erstwhile religious and farming community, now tranquil nature reserve Isola Polvese (Walk 12), also with accommodation.

Back on dry land, beyond the southeast edge of the shoreline, stretch mountainous elevations dotted with appealing little-visited villages. Humble Monte Penna is traversed in Walk 13, which drops fleetingly into the tiny settlements of Montemelino and Montesperello. A swing southwest and Monte Pausillo is the destination of Walk 14, which commences at attractive Paciano, while Monte Arale is 'summited' in Walk 15. A handy base is quiet Piegaro (with hotels and bus services from Perugia and Orvieto), nestling in woods. Delving into its fascinating history reveals it grew to be an enormously successful centre of glassmaking back in the 1200s, thanks to the arrival of skilled artisans from the Veneto; glass mosaics for the wonderful cathedrals of Orvieto, Perugia, Milano and Bologna were crafted here. Visitors can learn more in the local museum.

WALK 9
Tuoro and Monte Gualandro

Start/Finish	Ca' di Giano
Alternative start/finish	Tuoro railway station
Distance	12km; or 18.5km
Ascent/Descent	350m/350m
Difficulty	Grade 1–2
Walking time	2hr 45min; from railway station: 4hr 15min
Maps	Parco del Lago Trasimeno e Zone Limitrofe 1:25,000 Monte Merli Editrice or Camminare in Umbria 1:50,000 Trasimeno-Medio Tevere, Istituto Geografico Adriatico
Refreshments	Nothing en route so buy picnic supplies in Tuoro; there's a supermarket on the road from the station.
Public transport	Train to Tuoro.
Access	The hamlet Ca' di Giano is on the road to Sanguineto; roadside parking is possible, otherwise drive to Sanguineto and begin there.

Not far from the shore of Lago Trasimeno, this wonderfully scenic route follows the wooded rim around the natural amphitheatre enclosing Tuoro, the setting for a famous battle between the ancient Romans and Hannibal no less (see box). The walk is marked as M27, and follows clear lanes with frequent red/white paint markers. One section is in common with the 'Percorso Storico Archeologico della Battaglia' aka 'Sentiero Annibalico', the Hannibal Trail, an easy route along roads visiting battle sites with informative maps and information. Points of interest are marked as 'sosta'.

Alternative start/finish at Tuoro railway station
From the station follow the road signs for **Tuoro**. You are quickly led under the expressway then N towards the town. Not far after a supermarket fork left (W) on Via del Porto (believed to coincide with an ancient lake shoreline) and stick with this road. Past a couple of intersections, it reaches a tall Roman column belonging to '**Sosta 8**' (Point 8) on the Hannibal Archeological route. You

then head through fields to a T-junction and '**Sosta 4**', meeting the cypress-lined road to Sanguineto. Go left here for Ca' di Giano (45min).

The cypress-lined road to Sanguineto

From **Ca' di Giano** (273m) turn off the Sanguineto road and walk uphill due W. Straight ahead the modest castle on Monte Gualandro stands out ringed by castellated walls. A short way up, as the road curves left at a villa, leave it for the lane straight ahead, marked red/white M27. In the company of hedges at first, it proceeds uphill through an olive plantation, branching left (SW) at a marked junction through light woodland but with good views over the lake. At a house go right (NNW) on a good dirt road for the last leg up to **Monte Gualandro** (444m, 40min) and its curious castle. ▶

If closed, visitors will have to be content with admiring it from the outside.

Now head NW-NNE on the lane that snakes its way along the lightly wooded crest with wonderful views both sides: to Val di Chiana and the patchwork of fields and towns west, as well as the hills and lake landscape. After a clearing planted with olive trees comes a superbly placed isolated house, **Contea** (474m). The scenic way continues N for the most part, along the border between

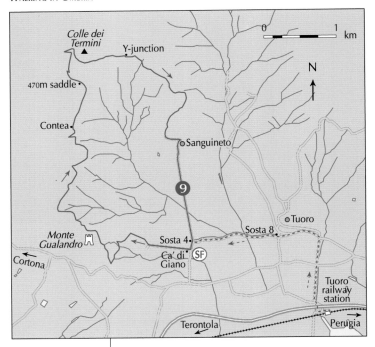

Tuscany and Umbria. At a five-way junction of lanes at a **saddle** (470m) M27 keeps straight on, climbing NW in wide curves. At a turn-off near a house at 536m, make sure you fork right (whereas an MTB route keeps left). Soon you are up on broad **Colle dei Termini** (550m) for a lovely strolling stretch due E with a vast outlook. An old stone border column dating back to 1757 is passed, and not far on you part company with the main ridge, as you need to branch right at a **Y-junction** (540m, 1hr 15min).

Looking over the battlefield site surrounded by wooded hills, the steady descent begins. It leads down to houses, tarmac and the handful of Agriturismo establishments that make up the quiet hamlet of **Sanguineto** (335m, 30min). Ignore the branch left for the Percorso

One of the information areas on the Hannibal Trail of archeological interest

Storico and go right. A quiet, delightful albeit surfaced road heads due S lined both sides with pencil straight cypress trees. It touches on points 6, 5 and 4 on the Hannibal Trail, before reaching **Ca' di Giano** (273m, 20min) once again.

HANNIBAL'S AMBUSH

Hannibal the charismatic general from Carthage had traversed Spain and the Alps and was intent on bringing his arch-enemies, the Romans, to their knees. On 21 June 217BC on the plain of Tuoro di Trasimeno, a mere spear's throw from Rome, he prepared a masterful ambush with an assortment of tribal soldiers and a single surviving elephant. Confused by the thick mist enveloping them, the Roman army led by Consul Flaminius Gaius came under lightning attack from troops hidden around the wooded slopes. The slaughter was staggering – 15,000 Romans fell with hardly time to draw their swords and 6000 were taken prisoner, compared to a 'mere' 1500 on Hannibal's side. Nowadays local place names serve as reminders: Ossaia for bones, Sanguineto for blood and Sepoltaglia for burial.

WALK 10

Passignano Ridge

Start/Finish	Passignano Municipio
Distance	15km
Ascent/Descent	500m/500m
Difficulty	Grade 2
Walking time	3hr 40min
Maps	Camminare in Umbria 1:50,000 Trasimeno-Medio Tevere, Istituto Geografico Adriatico
Refreshments	There are no eateries en route so take a picnic. Passignano has stacks of grocery shops.
Access	From the railway station it is a 5min walk into Passignano. The Municipio/Comune or Town Hall is in the main square, Piazza Trento e Trieste (also a car park), just off the main road and not far from the ferry landing stage.

Starting out close to the shores of Lago Trasimeno, this lovely loop walk heads up past the charming old medieval enclave of Passignano. Proceeding on easy lanes and paths with only brief stretches of surfaced road, it leads through olive groves and Mediterranean woodland to a magnificently scenic ridge overlooking the lake and vast swathes of Umbria. Well marked throughout with red/white stripes and M25, the walk coincides partly with local route n.5 as well as the yellow-marked Franciscan pilgrim way.

Passignano was originally an Etruscan settlement, although its name derives from Passum Jani, Pass of Janus, the Roman god depicted with two faces for past and future, beginnings and transitions.

On the opposite side of the square from the Municipio at **Passignano** (265m) is the Pro Loco office. ◄ Alongside this building take the steps marked M25 and 'Rocca medievale'. Not far up ignore the right-hand entrance for the Rocca and keep uphill on a narrow road outside the town walls. Markings soon point you left on Via della Rocca past scenically located houses with lake views. At a fork in the road with a mapboard, keep right (NE) on the lane through olive groves.

At the next junction veer left in the company of rows of cypress trees to the rambling buildings of **Villa Le Masse** (327m). Here gentle descent on a rough lane sees you curving SSE to a path fork left uphill through

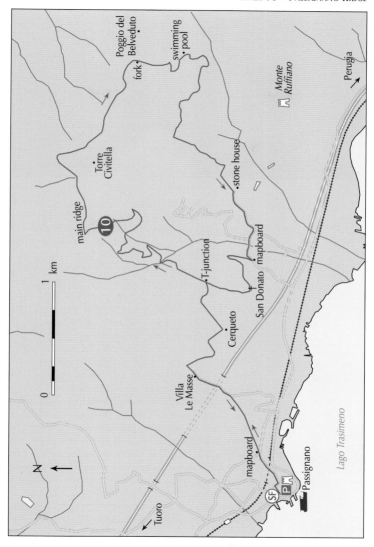

Poggio del Belveduto

swimming pool

fork

Torre Civitella

main ridge

10

T-junction

stone house

Monte Rufiano

Perugia

mapboard

San Donato

Cerqueto

Villa Le Masse

mapboard

Tuoro

Passignano

SF

P

Lago Trasimeno

N

1 km

0

67

rock roses and broom. Not far on are the small farms of **Cerqueto** and a minor road where you turn left uphill. The tarmac quickly peters out and a level lane leads into light woodland then across open grassland with a vast outlook. This reaches a **T-junction** (353m, 45min) with a lone cypress tree and buildings, where the return loop joins up afterwards. Branch left down a conifer-lined lane past a villa to pick up a lane that climbs in wide curves mostly N. After a house, the route enters woodland comprising tree heather, rock roses and aromatic shrubs all the way to the **main ridge** (558m, 40min).

Here go right on a broad unsurfaced road that snakes its panoramic way E. After skirting a hilltop property, **Torre Civitella**, you bear SE downhill. Further markings point you off the ridge at an abrupt right-hand fork (S) (513m, 25min), not far from **Poggio del Belveduto** and its farm. A muddy path cuts through to a rough lane downhill and past a small **swimming pool** soon followed by a horse riding establishment (both abandoned at the time of writing). At a clutch of houses M25 bears right (W) on a level at first to become a rocky muddy track dropping gradually through woodland frequented by boars, judging on the hoof prints. After a building you turn left onto a decent lane that overlooks orderly rows of olive trees around the curious conical hill of Monte Ruffiano (southeast) topped with a ruined tower. A charming square

stone house, beautifully located with lake views, marks the start of tarmac. Not far on a signed fork right leads through a built-up area where on Via Le Macce you fork sharp R (N) at a mapboard. Soon the unsurfaced way loops back on itself (SW) through olive groves to emerge at the modest church of **San Donato** (307m). Here fork right and next right again up a rutted lane leading to the T-junction (353m, 1hr 10min) and lone cypress tree encountered on the way out. Branch left now and retrace the way back to **Passignano** (265m, 40min).

WALK 11
Isola Maggiore

Start/Finish	Ferry wharf, Isola Maggiore
Distance	2.5km
Ascent/Descent	49m/49m
Difficulty	Grade 1
Walking time	1hr 10min
Maps	Parco del Lago Trasimeno e Zone Limitrofe 1:25,000 Monte Merli Editrice or Camminare in Umbria 1:50,000 Trasimeno-Medio Tevere, Istituto Geografico Adriatico
Refreshments	There is a good choice of cafés and restaurants on the island.
Access	Year-round ferries connect Tuoro, Castiglione and Passignano with the island.

On northwestern Lago Trasimeno, the peaceful, car-free island of Isola Maggiore boasts a picturesque fishing village, pretty walks through olive groves and along the wooded shoreline and surprising numbers of tame pheasants and rabbits. Despite its name (Isola Maggiore means 'largest island'), at a mere 800m in length, it comes in second to Isola Polvese (Walk 12).

It is well worth hopping on the ferry for the trip over the vast expanse of usually placid water. The easy walk can be followed by a lunch of tasty grilled lake fish, and visitors who wish to appreciate the islands' calm atmosphere for longer, can stay overnight at the modest hotel. At weekends and public holidays, however, the island can get busy.

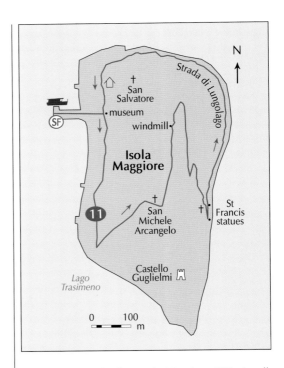

From the **ferry wharf** on Isola Maggiore (260m) walk
straight ahead to the island's modest museum on the village main street. Here turn right (S) past the rows of old
stone houses spread along the western shoreline. The
way quickly becomes a roughly paved lane that climbs
diagonally and decisively above the buildings. It is not far
to a fork left (straight ahead leads to Castello Guglielmi,
closed for long-term restoration) to the lookout and 15th-
century church **San Michele Arcangelo** (309m). Behind
the simple facade are some beautiful frescoes, should
you be lucky enough to find the place open. The highest point on the island, it offers lovely views between
the ancient cypress and olive trees to the mountainous
mainland.

Walk around the church to the Strada Panoramica del Molino and take this lovely scenic lane N past olive trees and giant fennel plants to a ruined *molino a vento* (windmill). Not far on is a junction where you branch right on Viale Marchesa Isabella, and walk the short distance to the turn-off left for Strada di San Francesco, with criss-cross fencing. This zigzags down to a Y-junction and shrine – go right on steps down to the shorefront with a trickling fountain and evocative weathered wood **St Francis statue** at the spot he is believed to have landed one stormy night in 1211. Nearby is a newer bronze statue and benches.

Now turn left along the **Strada di Lungolago**, a delightful promenade dotted with picnic benches, to the island's northernmost promontory. As the way veers S towards the village, ignore the flight of steps to San Salvatore and wander through the village with its vegetable gardens, tidy stone houses with fishing craft moored at the doorsteps, not to mention the hotel and restaurants. As you reach the **museum**, fork right back to the ferry wharf.

Looking back to Passignano from the ferry

WALK 12
Isola Polvese

Start/Finish	Ferry wharf, Isola Polvese
Distance	3.5km
Ascent/Descent	65m/65m
Difficulty	Grade 1
Walking time	1hr
Maps	Parco del Lago Trasimeno e Zone Limitrofe 1:25,000 Monte Merli Editrice or Camminare in Umbria 1:50,000 Trasimeno-Medio Tevere, Istituto Geografico Adriatico
Refreshments	Café-restaurant near the wharf.
Access	From Easter to October ferries run to the island regularly from San Feliciano and occasionally from Passignano. Isola Polvese cannot be visited the rest of the year.

Peaceful Isola Polvese, in the middle of Lago Trasimeno, was once home to half a dozen monasteries and churches and 500 people who lived by fishing and the cultivation of olives and wheat from 12th to the 16th centuries. Nowadays a mere handful of inhabitants tend organic olive groves, visitors and study groups. The Province of Perugia has seen fit to establish a nature reserve, a haven for hundreds of birds happily at home in the thickets of reeds.

The easy stroll around the gentle hills and shores of this well-kept island park makes for a leisurely outing, which can be stretched into a day by branching off on the other island paths, as well as indulging in lunch. Accommodation is also available.

From the **ferry wharf** on Isola Polvese walk straight head towards the elegant yellow pastel villa which doubles as a café-restaurant, and branch left along the lane. Not far on are the ruins of a 15th-century **castle**, which make for an interesting visit.

Continue along the lane NW amid poplars and parallel to the water's edge. Ignore the first branch right and keep on to where the lane bears right (NE) diagonally uphill through olive groves. Up on the **central ridge** at a

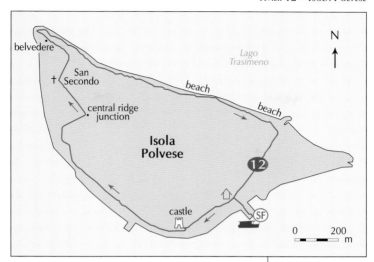

junction take the left turn to the photogenic church-mon-astery of **San Secondo** and its clucking jackdaw colony. The avenue-lane proceeds in gentle descent N and you

Passing the ruined castle on peaceful Isola Polvese

soon fork left. Not far on as the way curves left, leave it and go straight ahead through a park **belvedere** (30min) smothered with rosemary bushes. There are benches here to sit and enjoy the wonderful views over the lake.

At the far end go down the steps to the island's north-western point, then turn right following the northern perimeter shaded by wood of holm oaks and bright with cyclamens. Modest beach areas are touched on before you bear S past playing fields back to the villa and ferry wharf (30min).

WALK 13

Montemelino and Montesperello

Start/Finish	Montemelino
Distance	6.5km
Ascent/Descent	260m/260m
Difficulty	Grade 2
Walking time	2hr 10min
Maps	Camminare in Umbria 1:50,000 Trasimeno-Medio Tevere, Istituto Geografico Adriatico
Refreshments	Montemelino has a café.
Public transport	There are no helpful buses; a car is essential.
Access	Montemelino is 8km southeast of Magione, and well signposted due to its well-visited 'Santuario della Madonna di Lourdes' church. Parking is plentiful.

This fine walk touches on quiet hillside villages set back from the southeastern corner of Lago Trasimeno. On tracks shared with trail bikers and mountain bikers, it climbs through woods to a superb lookout over the lake and the cultivated hinterland. Corresponding to a slice of the M21 itinerary, it has reliable red/white waymarking.

On the uphill side of the church at **Montemelino** (341m) is a signpost for the 'M21'. This points initially SW on a narrow road, then it forks first right, climbing steeply

The path through Mediterranean wood on Monte Penna

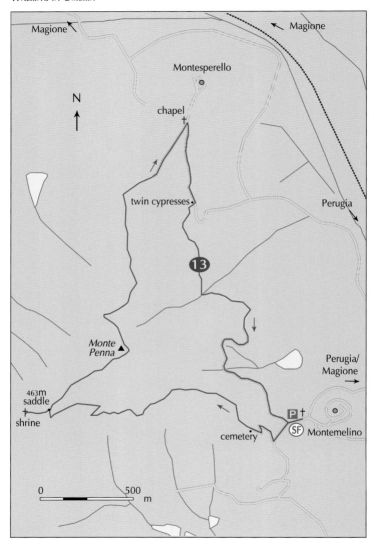

to the **cemetery** and the end of the tarmac. A wide path continues initially N over sandy terrain into woodland where red/white waymarks need to be followed closely. As it bears W, the vegetation thins allowing views to open up nicely over wooded hill and cultivated vale. Further uphill a **saddle** (463m, 35min) and power pylon are easily gained. However, before taking a breather, branch sharp left up to a shrine (480m) with a welcoming bench.

> The **view** from the shrine is a wide one. Due west on Lago Trasimeno is Isola Polvese, northwest is the sprawl of Magione, Perugia lies east, while below at the base of the hill runs the 'emissario' lake drainage channel excavated by the ancient Etruscan to manage the water level.

Return to the saddle (10min) and continue on a wide path straight ahead (NE) into the trees on 490m **Monte Penna**, the actual peak elusive. ▶ Continue N-NW winding down in shady woodland. At a brick building and track junction keep left; Montesperello comes into sight below, backed by the plains. Soon a singularly steep and rutted but thankfully short section plunges to a good lane. Branch right here and, not far on, a quiet surfaced road leads downhill to a **chapel** located at an intersection (321m, 45min). Close at hand is the elongated shoulder that is home to the stately manor houses of **Montesperello**, a brief optional detour.

As the descent begins, it's best to ignore the markers for 'Circuito MTB Trekking' as while they shortcut a corner or two, they can lead walkers astray!

Branch right (S) downhill on the narrow road. Some 5min on, M21 forks right onto a lane between huge twin cypresses for a gentle ascent past olive groves then light wood. Keep an eye out for red/white waymarks at the many turnoffs. The way becomes stonier and steeper, reaching a rise where olive trees reappear. Keep straight ahead to where a lane veers right and the village of Montemelino comes into sight. A couple of small farms are passed then a wide lane follows the contours of a side valley back to the saddle and church of **Montemelino** (341m, 40min).

WALK 14

Paciano and Monte Pausillo

Start/Finish	Paciano park
Distance	11km
Ascent/Descent	440m/440m
Difficulty	Grade 2
Walking time	3hr
Maps	Camminare in Umbria 1:50,000 Trasimeno-Medio Tevere, Istituto Geografico Adriatico or Parco del Lago Trasimeno e Zone Limitrofe 1:25,000 Monte Merli Editrice
Refreshments	Picnic supplies can be bought in Paciano, or eat at Agriturismo Miralaghi (tel 348 3701085).
Public transport	Buses from Perugia and Castiglione del Lago serve the village.
Access	By car it is a short detour off the SS71, south of Lago Trasimeno. The public park where the walk starts is near the northernmost gate Porta Fiorentina, close to the main church. Roadside car parking is possible.

Views over the wonderful Umbrian and Tuscan countryside are plentiful on this easy if longish walk that follows lanes, roads and paths along brilliantly panoramic ridges. It begins at the appealing village of Paciano, almost entirely constructed in red brick – defensive walls and streets included. En route waymarking is fairly frequent – red/white M29.

From the park at **Paciano** (467m) walk along Viale Roma keeping the tall brick walls on your left. Leaving the village behind, keep right past old wash troughs and a sign for 'M29', and downhill on the road to a **church**. Fork left here onto what soon becomes a dirt lane heading NW between rural properties and olive groves. It descends to a sunken lane lined with hedgerows and passes a couple of houses. A lane flanking fields and a **machinery yard** leads to tarmac – turn left onto this for the uphill scenic stretch. Just after a cluster of houses called **Varacca**, fork right onto an unsurfaced road curving past **Pietreto** (378m) and its olive trees. Soon you branch left (S) onto asphalt that soon reverts to a lane on its steep way up to

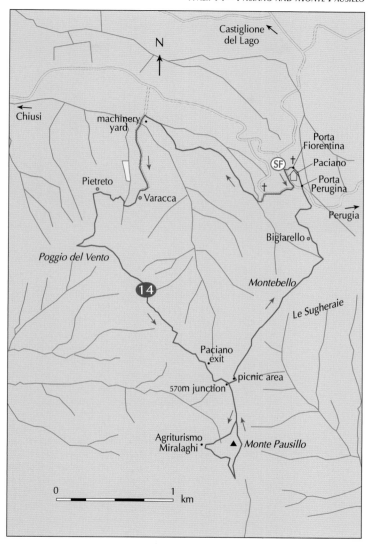

Castiglione
del Lago

N

Chiusi

machinery
yard

Porta
Fiorentina

SF

Paciano

Porta
Perugina

Pietreto

Varacca

Perugia

Bigiarello

Poggio del Vento

Montebello

14

Le Sugheraie

Paciano
exit

picnic area

570m junction

Agriturismo
Miralaghi

Monte Pausillo

0   1   km

Paciano and its imposing walls

a saddle on the edge of a pine plantation on **Poggio del Vento**.

Bearing left (SE), the ascent is gentler and the views take in vast cultivated plains extending to Lago Trasimeno. Amid rock roses, broom and carpets of orchids continue past horse riding farms – ignore the fork left for Paciano unless an early exit is needed. Keep on past the Villa Lidia property to a **junction** (570m, 1hr 40min) where the return route breaks off. By staying on the lane S you reach **Agriturismo Miralaghi** (577m, 10min). True to its name 'lakeview', its superb outlook takes in both Chiusi and Trasimeno, without neglecting Monte Cetona and the perfect volcanic cone of Monte Amiata to the west.

Turn left now (M29) on a scenic lane then left again (N) around **Monte Pausillo** and past its radio masts. Soon back on the outward way, retrace your steps to the 570m junction (10min) and branch right up to a **picnic area** and pine wood. Go left into the wood and follow the marks very carefully through the trees to a clear track carpeted with pine needles. A photogenic 'avenue' of conifers leads down to a saddle. Here ignore the sign left and go straight ahead on the clear ridge path NE

The avenue of conifers during the descent

This area is known as Le Sugheraie for its concentration of cork oaks.

towards **Montebello**. ◄ Mediterranean vegetation dominates a little longer, then a fork left marks the start of the descent into chestnut wood. After touching on **Bigiarello**, you quickly reach charming Paciano and enter via **Porta Perugina**. Walk along the main street through the piazza then take Via Marconi and out through **Porta Fiorentina** to the park (1hr).

WALK 15
Monte Arale

Start/Finish	Montarale park
Distance	13km
Ascent/Descent	400m/400m
Difficulty	Grade 2
Walking time	3hr
Maps	Camminare in Umbria 1:50,000 Trasimeno-Medio Tevere, Istituto Geografico Adriatico
Refreshments	Take your own picnic from Piegaro, or stop at café-restaurant La Baita del Montarale (tel 349 7245755 weekends).
Public transport	While Piegaro is accessible by bus from Perugia and Orvieto, a car is essential for reaching the walk start.
Access	Below the northeastern edge of Piegaro a sign for 'Montarale' points uphill for a highly scenic 5.5km drive. It passes through a string of hamlets, the last of which is Pratalanza, after which the way narrows rather, becoming twisty and steeper. There are spacious car parks at Montarale.

This is a lovely half-day walk in a triangular route on and around Monte Arale, which looms southeast above the village of Piegaro. (Note: the park is called Montarale.) The topmost part is flattish open moorland with tree heather, broom and conifer, cloaked in moss and colourful lichens, which thrive here in great numbers thanks to the mists that often shroud the mountain. Walkers should be aware that after rain many of the lanes will be muddy. On the other hand, waymarking is easy to follow – stick to the red/white M17, and ignore all others.

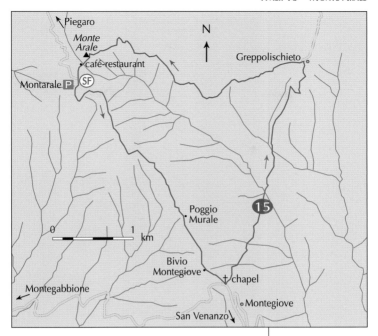

At **Montarale** (853m), go right on the lane marked red/
white M17. This soon forks left downhill into light wood
which luckily manages not to obstruct the vast views.
Following waymarked forks carefully, it is SSE along a
lane and over a rise thick with cypress trees. A gentle scenic descent ensues, with Montegabbione standing out on
its hill perch to the west. Further down, at a junction on
Poggio Murale looking towards the castle-like village of
Montegiove, leave the lane for a clear path left, signed
for **Bivio Montegiove**, a reference point located further
down. Once at the roadside and a **chapel** (564m, 1hr)
close to the foot of the afore-mentioned village, turn left
(NNE) along a quiet unmade road.

Fields of thriving cereal crops line the way, and you
dip across two watercourses, followed by a gentle climb

The walk goes through the peaceful hamlet of Greppolischieto

flanked with old stone walls past farms to the sleepy hamlet of **Greppolischieto** (628m, 1hr). Wander through the tiny settlement and exit by the front portal – close by is a perfectly appointed bench, an ideal spot for a picnic with vast views to Lago Trasimeno due north.

Then go left (W) on an unmade road but soon fork left for the return climb on a rough lane through light wood. This is the picture all the way up to the huge cross on **Monte Arale** (853m), where a wonderful panorama can be enjoyed. Continue via the summer café-restaurant and picnic area back to **Montarale park** (1hr).

3 ORVIETO AND TODI

Orvieto's glittering cathedral was built to house a miraculous relic (Walk 18)

INTRODUCTION

In southwest Umbria, Orvieto is located above the major Florence–Rome valley and transport artery. But it stands aloof, unaffected by the frenetic traffic. An awesome raft of honey-coloured tufa rock supports the atmospheric town, made up of a medieval maze of streets and a glittering cathedral that stands out gloriously for miles. Site of the wealthy 6th–4th century BC Etruscan city of Velzna, sacked and razed to the ground by the Romans in 294BC, it was rebuilt, renamed 'Urbs vetus' old city (Orvieto), and went on to prosper fantastically throughout the Renaissance. It can be reached by train (Orvieto Scalo station) followed by a short funicular or bus trip, and is an excellent base. Walk 16 and 17 investigate the immediate surrounds, while Walk 18 takes an old pilgrim route across to Lago di Bolsena.

To the east, exploring the untamed hills around Lago di Corbara and accessible from Orvieto are Walks 19, 20 and 21. The first two begin at the secluded timeless medieval hamlet of Titignano where a sojourn is possible (and the rare bus calls in), while Walk 21 begins at Civitella del Lago, a marvellous village-cum-belvedere with a family-run *locanda* and regular bus

Looking out from the square in Titignano (Walks 19 and 20)

Consolazione in Todi, where the buses terminate

services. Both overlook lovely Lago di Corbara, formed 1959–1962 when a dam was thrown across the River Tiber where it swerves south on its way to Rome.

A short way upstream, lofty Todi stands out like a lighthouse on an isolated conical hill, visible for miles and miles across the rolling countryside. The particularly vertical site was chosen by an eagle, no less, as depicted in the town's insignia. Swooping low, he carried off a red cloth belonging to men from the 8th-century BC colony, setting it high on the hilltop and interpreted as a divine sign. Standing at a strategic confluence of roads and watercourses, Todi became a key trade centre. However, over the centuries it has been subject to ongoing landslides caused by water infiltrating the thick layers of clay underlying the sediments on which it was built, combated since at least Roman times by excavating underground drainage channels. Well served by buses, it also has rail links to Terni and Perugia thanks to the Ponte Rio station (FCU railway) at the bottom of the hill. Walk 22 begins in Todi, while Walk 23 explores the countryside a short distance away.

WALK 16
Orvieto ring walk

Start/Finish	Upper funicular station, Piazza Cahen, Orvieto
Distance	6km
Ascent/Descent	200m/200m
Difficulty	Grade 1
Walking time	1hr 45min, plus 45min for Necropoli visit
Maps	Orvieto town map from the Tourist Office in Piazza Duomo
Refreshments	Cafés in Piazza Cahen and grocery shops in Orvieto.
Access	Piazza Cahen is located on the eastern edge of town, and serves as the terminal for the funicular and buses from Orvieto Scalo railway station lower down.

Below wonderful Orvieto, at the foot of the soaring cliffs of the town's rock platform, this *anello della rupe* (ring of the rock) takes a clear pedestrian way, relaxing and enjoyable thanks to EU-funded cliff consolidation work. As you stroll the route, wonderful views open up across the surrounding hills overlaid with olive groves, woodland and farms, while a string of information boards provides fascinating historical detail.

It can be completed in under two hours but by allowing half a day you can take several recommended detours to Etruscan sites, and linger around other points of interest. The walk can be joined or left at many different points, mentioned en route.

Before starting the circuit, from Piazza Cahen, pop into the gardens of Fortezza Albornoz to enjoy some excellent views.

◄ At **Piazza Cahen**, turn sharp left downhill on the black stone paved lane that leaves the town via **Porta Soliana**, plunging downhill to curve left and over the funicular. At the first bend, fork left around a gate onto a surfaced lane close to the cliff base where evidence of the extensive consolidation can be seen. Keep left at the next fork, then as this lane peters out, go right to rejoin the lower way W through light woodland, following arrows for 'percorso rupe'. It climbs gently to cross the main road near the **Grotta della Fungaia**, an old cave formerly used for mushroom cultivation. Continuing beneath sheer cliffs it

is not far to the turn-off right for the **Necropoli Etrusca Crocifisso del tufo**. Well worth the modest entry charge, this fascinating 'city of the dead' comprises narrow streets lined with square room-like tombs bearing the occupants' family name.

The walk leaves the town precincts via Porta Soliana

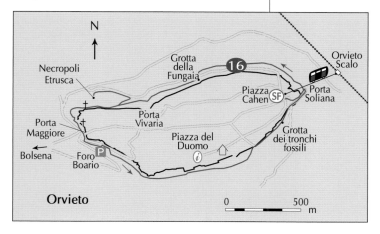

89

*The Etruscan Necropolis of
Crocifisso del tufo*

Turn left into the town up Via della Cava to visit the amazing Pozzo della Cava, Etruscan well (10min there and back).

Afterwards return uphill to resume the main route near the walkway from **Porta Vivaria** (alternate access/exit). Keep right (W) high above the necropolis with views over the countryside, and past a tiny rock chapel with an image of Christ ostensibly carved out of the rock by the bare hands of a sixth-century soldier in thanks for protection. Not far around the corner is the white church Madonna del Velo then **Porta Maggiore** (45min), an another important town entry/exit point. ◄

Staying outside the walls-cum-cliffs, you soon cross the road right to drop to the Foro Boario car park. Keep left past the *scala mobile* (escalator) and *ascensore* (lift) that provide access to the upper town. Continue SE past the archways with sections of the old aqueduct (see Walk 17) and on through through a small car park. Ignore the steep descent right and keep straight on around a gate then a corner lined with giant rushes to parkland. A signboard explains the presence of the many artificial caves and dovecotes, important to the Romans who bred the birds for food. Soon fork left uphill to the cliff base then keep right (E). On the coming stretch you can admire the photogenic abbey of SS Severio e Martirio across the valley. A gentle downhill leads past another access/exit to town (for Palazzo Crispo Marsciano, close to Piazza Duomo) then joins a black paved lane uphill beneath a rockface where chattering jackdaws and crows nest in chinks, as well as wallflowers and straggly caper plants. After a cave with fossilised tree trunks (**Grotta dei tronchi fossili**) comes a sharp left turn back up through **Porta Soliana** and **Piazza Cahen** (1hr).

WALK 17
Orvieto Aqueduct loop

Start/Finish	Foro Boario car park, Orvieto
Distance	6km
Ascent/Descent	270m/270m
Difficulty	Grade 1–2
Walking time	2hr
Maps	Photographic route map from the Tourist Office in Piazza Duomo
Refreshments	Nothing en route
Access	Foro Boario car park is located on the lower southwest side of town, and can be reached from Orvieto by the escalator and lift.

A rewarding walk on the outskirts of town follows the medieval aqueduct. Dating back to the mid-1300s, the imposing construction was designed to convey much-needed water to Orvieto from the Alfina uplands. Unfortunately the project proved troublesome, with leakages being a common problem, and eventually fell into disrepair to be replaced by rainwater cisterns. Amazingly a long stretch has survived to this day and, from the southern edge of the township, is still clearly visible with an accompanying straight line of trees. With both uphill and downhill stretches, the walk meanders through lovely countryside and occasional overgrown tracts, and a high ridge that boasts what are arguably the best views of Orvieto. Further interest comes in the shape of modest Etruscan tombs and the Campo della Fiera archeological site towards the end.

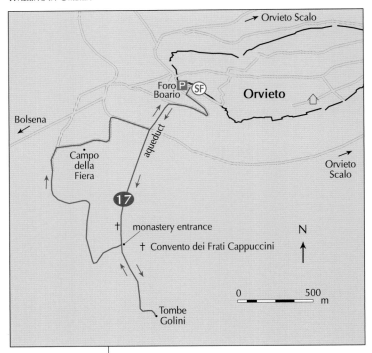

From the *cassa* (cashier booth) at **Foro Boario** (260m), cross the car park and take the steps down to join the road out of town. This means turning left along the tarmac and following it around the first bend. Then, not far downhill fork left on Strada di Portaromana (marked red/white n.6), a lane that plunges SW past a house to quickly reach the first stretch of aqueduct. Continuing in the same direction, the route crosses a busy road (190m) to an information board where the aqueduct itself towers overhead. A little way on, as the gravel lane veers right into private property, keep straight ahead on a faint path that is occasionally overgrown. It is a steady climb due S into woodland dominated by oak and ivy where from time to time the original shiny black basalt paving stones appear underfoot (*selciato* in Italian).

At a large cross, a track lined with cypress trees breaks off left to a chapel – ignore it and proceed alongside a wall to a white gravel lane and the official entrance to the **Convento dei Frati Cappuccini** (50min); this is also where the return route forks off. The lane leads uphill before levelling out past a house. Take the first turn left then fork immediately right to the **Tombe Golini** (394m, 1hr).

> Long corridors lead to the **burial chambers**, once decorated with colourful frescoes and now on display in the town's Museo Archeologico Nazionale. The tombs are also referred to as the Tombe Settecamini or Hescania, for the noble family to whom they belonged. From the picnic tables enjoy the superb views to glorious Orvieto and its cathedral.

A sublime view back to the city

Backtrack to the monastery entrance and fork left on the white gravel lane that curves downhill SW at first past a property with olive trees in a field. The way then bears N with views across the cultivated valley, while the ochre dome of the cemetery stands out beyond. Continue down to a surfaced road and go right past a couple of houses. Immediately after a yellow electricity substation tower, branch right on a narrow asphalted way leading through to Campo della Fiera.

> **Campo della Fiera**, a former key Etruscan sanctuary, Roman settlement and market place, is currently being excavated by archeologists and is fenced off, however original Roman paving and outlines of buildings can be seen.

Proceed on past a small factory, then turn left towards the main road. Branch right along the busy asphalt with care for 5min to the aqueduct once more. Then turn left for the steepish climb back to **Foro Boario** (260m, 1hr).

WALK 18
Orvieto to Bolsena

Start/Finish	Porta Maggiore, Orvieto/Piazza Santa Cristina, Bolsena
Distance	15.6km
Ascent/Descent	440m/380m
Difficulty	Grade 2
Walking time	4hr
Maps	Orvietano e Trasimeno 1:50,000 Istituto Geografico Adriatico
Refreshments	Take food and drink as no cafés or shops are encountered until Bolsena.
Public transport	At Bolsena catch the bus (Mon–Sat) to return to Orvieto.
Access	Porta Maggiore is on the southwestern edge of Orvieto, near the Foro Boario car park. From the town centre take Via della Cava out through the massive walls.

This walk retraces the route of a procession that took place in the 13th century, although in reverse direction (to fit in with the bus schedule for the return). After a steepish climb out of Orvieto it wanders across open scenic countryside and swathes of wooded tableland, before descending to the placid lake. Waymarking en route – red/white paint splashes and 4f – tends to be patchy, so directions need to be followed closely. A torch is handy for the Etruscan tombs en route.

A CLEAR MESSAGE

In 1293 a solemn procession made its way from the village of Bolsena on the shores of Italy's largest volcanically formed lake across the hills to the proud medieval township of Orvieto. It bore a precious relic – a blood-stained altar cloth – to be placed in the magnificent glittering cathedral constructed specially to house it. The background? To cut a long story short, a Bohemian priest in pilgrimage to Rome was assailed by terrible doubts about transubstantiation. When he paused to say mass in the chapel of revered early Christian martyr Santa Cristina, blood began to drip from the host wafer onto the altar cloth. A clear message to him! Pope Urban IV proclaimed a miracle and instituted the catholic feast of Corpus Domini, celebrated faithfully and widely with flower-decorated streets.

From **Porta Maggiore** (260m) turn right then first left downwards on Strada Dritta del Marchigiano, where you will see red/white waymarking. At the bottom of the hill go right then left onto Strada dell'Arcone then right for Via della Gabelletta. This quickly leads down across the stone bridge **Ponte del Sole** (184m, 20min), its shrine commemorating the 13th-century procession. Now the main road bears right towards the cypress-ringed cemetery, but you continue straight ahead (SW) through **Tamburino**. This stretch follows a minor road climbing steadily through peaceful countryside where olives and grapes flourish.

The way reverts to original dark basalt cobblestones, and narrows to a path. The **SS71** Orvieto–Bolsena road is crossed (1hr) and you proceed through shady woodland to the curious **Sassotagliato** 'cut rock' passage (424m),

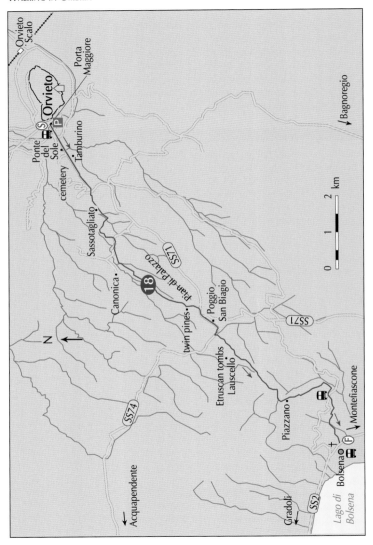

Leaving Orvieto behind

ostensibly where the rock miraculously split open to allow for the passage of the procession. An old bridge is passed then several caves. The route heads SW on a sunken lane overhung with sweet chestnut trees and oak, flanking a watercourse and fields. This soon takes a sharp right out of the wood to embark on a short westward loop. Follow the red/white stripes and stay on the lane over a rise. Then, after farms and a stream, fork left, soon reaching a minor road.

Follow this right, past houses and through rolling farming countryside for 5min to where a signposted lane branches left. Heading SW once more, accompanied by thick hedgerows, you pass rural properties, while across west the picturesque hamlet of Canonica is visible. Do not be tempted by the numerous turn-offs, but stick to the main track. After a climb bordered by grape vines, woodland takes over, followed by a beautiful longish stretch through open fields, almost English countryside. This area is known as the **Pian di Palazzo** (550m).

At prominent **twin pines** (1hr) comes a marked curve left (S) out to the main road **SS71** once more. Keep right on a parallel minor road for about 1km past **Poggio San**

Under protective roofing are modest underground chambers accessible by way of steep crumbly steps and a corridor.

Biagio (591m) then after the broad curve downhill protected by a guard rail, take the first track off left (signposted) between fields crammed with sunflowers. Be sure to leave this the moment it curves left, for the rougher lane straight ahead in light woods. A brief climb away is a series of modest Etruscan tombs not far from **Lauscello** (30min). ◀

You soon join a wider track on the edge of open fields planted with maize, maintaining a constant SW direction. From a crest at 620m, the lake comes into sight in all its glittering glory.

> Backed by the Monti Volsini **Lago di Bolsena** appears as an immense expanse of water, watched over by the township of Capodimonte on the opposite shore. Twin islands seem to brood or float, depending on light and weather conditions.

Overlooking the valley of Fosso del Ponticello the lane soon veers right, ignoring a ruined house (Podere dei Preti). Keep left then a short way uphill left again, branching S. At a house a wider track is joined for a pleasant stretch uphill past a property (**Piazzano**, 583m). With the lake clearly visible southwest, follow a stately tree-lined avenue as it winds to the road and a bus stop (502m, 1hr).

Not far downhill turn left on a steep narrow road, with a traffic sign '*escluso residenti*' (except residents) but walkers can proceed without a problem. This handy short cut drops quickly past a church on the lower flanks of the ancient volcanic crater, now a curious crag honeycombed with caves and tunnels used as storage and hutches. You finally arrive in **Bolsena** proper and Piazza Santa Cristina (347m, 30min).

Across the square, alias erstwhile Roman forum, is the 12th-century church with the Cappella del Miracolo and the wondrous stone imprinted by the saint's feet, as well as fourth-century catacombs. The bus stop is a short stroll right, below the grey stone buildings of the old district.

WALK 19
Titignano Loop

Start/Finish	Titignano car park
Distance	13.5km
Ascent/Descent	450m/450m
Difficulty	Grade 2–3
Walking time	4hr 30min
Maps	Parco Fluviale del Tevere 1:25,000 Monte Merli Edtrice
Refreshments	None available.
Public transport	Mon–Sat buses between Orvieto and Todi stop at Titignano, but not at helpful times for walkers.
Access	Titignano is at the end of a 3km unmade branch road off the scenic SS79bis connecting Orvieto and Todi.

Starting at the charming hamlet of Titignano, which has a restaurant and accommodation but nowhere to buy a picnic, this rewarding but long loop makes its way towards the banks of Lago di Corbara. The area belongs to the Parco Fluviale del Tevere (River Tiber Park) and is home to abundant porcupine judging from the quills, and armies of wild boar judging from the muddy hoof marks. Pheasants are easy to see and hear, and birds of prey circle overhead.

While the walk begins and ends on good lanes, the middle section takes very narrow paths through dense Mediterranean woodland where orientation is tricky and waymarking patchy to say the least – so special care is needed in following directions. Walk 20 is shorter and more straightforward.

From the **car park** at the war memorial of Titignano (521m), walk along the paved lane lined with cypress trees. At the end, without entering the charming village square, fork right down a lane that passes under a footbridge next to the awesome wall of the castle. The hamlet is quickly left behind as you head NW past a handful of rural properties and farmland. ▶

The way descends gently into shrub cover of Mediterranean plants including rock roses and broom. After a couple of curves, at a small clearing (380m, 40min), as the white gravel lane bears W leave it for a

Views range over the rolling wooded hills that slope down to the lakeside as well as the landmark village of Prodo on its ridge west.

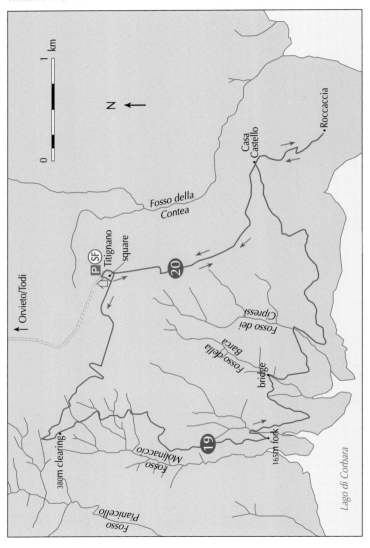

rougher track mostly S. It dips and climbs over rises and through muddy sections, soon giving brilliant lake views. About 20min on, on an open rise, fork right (a sign on a tree for 'n.7'). A faint but wide track plunges down a grassy hillside dotted with broom and fennel plants, soon reaching a saddle where a red n.8 points sharp right.

Follow the consecutive numbers to a stony lane not far from the water's edge (**165m fork**). Now ignore the red numbers and go left through alternating rushes and woodland, in and out, up and down, essentially heading E. Ruins of a red brick building mark a small **bridge** over Fosso della Barca, followed by an overgrown stone wall and abandoned olive groves. Soon at a lane junction fork right (white arrow n.9) to cross nearby **Fosso dei Cipressi**, easily recognisable by the many cypress trees and conifers.

In damp wood now the lane continues S (unlike the route shown on the 1:25000 map) to a clearing with white crumbly rock. Go left as per white arrow 10, then 11 and 12. At arrow 13, fork right for a narrow path, then at 14 fork sharp left to start climbing and curving NW up to a junction at 380m. Now fork right (arrow 15) and

A lovely picnic spot overlooking Lago di Corbara

This is a fine spot to view Titignano as well as the city of Todi, in the northeast.

it is finally out of the wood (past arrows 16 and 17) to a lane on an open broad ridge at **Casa Castello** (404m, 2hr 30min), an abandoned house with its own well. ◀

Turn left (initially NW) up the wide gravel lane (way-marked 5b) flanking vineyards and fields and hedgerows, and accompanied by vast views over Lago di Corbara. Keep right at a junction then curve uphill with cypress trees. The lane circles behind the church and returns to the car park at **Titignano** (1hr).

WALK 20
Titignano to Roccaccia

Start/Finish	Titignano car park
Distance	7km
Ascent/Descent	150m/150m
Difficulty	Grade 1
Walking time	2hr
Maps	Parco Fluviale del Tevere 1:25,000 Monte Merli Edtrice
Refreshments	None available.
Public transport	Mon–Sat buses between Orvieto and Todi stops at Titignano, but not at helpful times for walkers.
Access	Titignano is at the end of a 3km unmade branch road off the scenic SS79bis connecting Orvieto and Todi.

From the tranquil hamlet of Titignano (restaurant and accommodation but nowhere to buy food) in its commanding position high above the north bank of Lago di Corbara, this straightforward and extremely pleasant walk follows wide lanes that ensure vast views across the hills of eastern Umbria. The route is marked with yellow/red/yellow lozenges and n.5b.

For route map see Walk 19.

◀ From the **car park** at the war memorial of Titignano (521m), walk along the paved lane lined with cypress trees and into the photogenic square. This features a stone church, homes and the old castle-cum-villa, which is now an atmospheric inn. At the far end of the square is

a lovely lookout to the lake and over the rolling hills, clad in Mediterranean wood. Here go left to join the lane that came direct from the car park. Turn right onto it to head S in gentle descent past a vast vineyard, La Vigna.

Right from the word go, the lane offers vast views. Ignore turn-offs and keep on downhill in the company of hedgerows, woodland and cultivated fields including more grape vines. The way bears gradually left (E) to reach the marvellous broad open saddle with sadly abandoned buildings of **Casa Castello** (404m), complete with its own well. ▶ Continue on to the signed fork right for a path through to the ruin of **Roccaccia** (411m, 1hr), a belvedere directly over the Gole del Forello, where the River Tiber is squeezed between cliffs.

Retrace your steps afterwards back up to Titignano. Once you reach the edge of the village, stick to the lane as its skirts the rear of the church, leading directly to the car park (1hr).

The tranquil hamlet of Titignano occupies a commanding position

This spot has an especially beautiful outlook to the city of Todi on its outcrop.

WALK 21
Civitella del Lago

Start/Finish	Civitella del Lago car park
Distance	11km
Ascent/Descent	400m/400m
Difficulty	Grade 2
Walking time	3hr 30min
Maps	Parco Fluviale del Tevere 1:25,000 Monte Merli Editrice
Refreshments	Groceries and fresh bread for picnics can be purchased in Civitella, which also boasts a scenic café-restaurant.
Public transport	Daily buses from Orvieto and Todi pass this way.
Access	By car take the SS448 and the branch off for Civitella del Lago. Once at the village, follow signs for 'centro' and stop in the large car park just before the main gated entrance.

This walk makes for a wonderful day's outing. It starts out at the laid-back medieval village of Civitella del Lago (with a lovely B&B), perched on a high ridge and well worth exploring, and meanders through woods and farmland with fine outlooks across the hills of Umbria that embrace many landmark towns. However, the main attraction is the vast spread of Lago di Corbara, where the flow of the River Tiber has been partially damned. Clear lanes and paths are taken but waymarking is scarce and faint. As long as directions are followed carefully at the many junctions, it should be a straightforward amble.

From the **car park** at Civitella del Lago (476m) walk out to the main crossroads and keep straight ahead ENE, passing the **cemetery**. At a large shrine go straight ahead on a lane (sign for 'Sentieri del Parco') past olive groves but soon turn left at the first turn-off past a picnic area. You ascend gently N through holm oak wood with clearings offering views back to Civitella del Lago and the lovely spread of the lake. In **Valle Spinosa**, accompanied by thickets of perfumed broom bushes, the way levels out, passing a couple of farms looking towards distant Todi to the north. A downhill section alongside olive trees

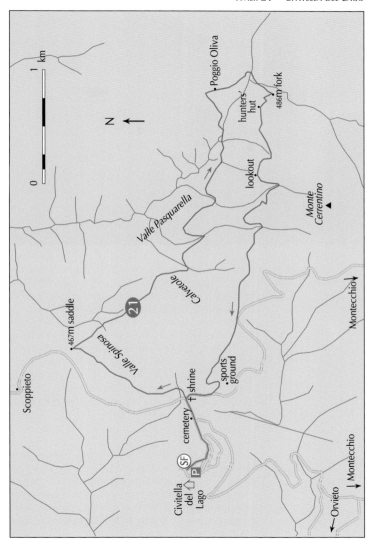

The route begins at Civitella del Lago

reaches a **467m saddle** (30min) that looks over to the village of Scoppieto. Fork right (SE) (ignoring the park arrow indicating straight on) through fields and into light woodland. At the ensuing fork 10min on, go left.

Ignoring minor turn-offs, follow the increasingly rough stony lane under an electricity line then dipping through an area of felled trees (**Calvetole**). Up the other side it soon enters a damp shady wooded valley where cyclamens brighten the undergrowth, and climbs gently SE, although with non-stop ups and downs. The way narrows to a clear path with occasional plunging views north into **Valle Pasquarella** below while the limestone base becomes more obvious, and red/white waymarks – albeit faded – appear.

A stream is forded in the vicinity of a modest canyon and uphill, not much further on, is a saddle with a manhole for the *acquedotto* (water mains). Here the red/white path veers right up onto a rock base dotted with rock roses and globeflowers. At a fork with a wider path, go right flanking a property with olive trees to the junction at **Poggio Oliva** (461m, 1hr). Branch right – ignoring the lane into a field – and soon descend to cross a stream, bearing right (SW). The rocky path with faded waymarks climbs through masses of broom, and it is not far up to a **486m fork** where you go right (W) winding up through wood thick with tree heather. This emerges amid shrubs cut back drastically by the hunters who frequent the tiny hut-cum-hide in a lovely panoramic position (544m).

A wider lane now continues W through chestnut wood and past other huts on the northern flanks of **Monte Cerrentino**. Further along are picnic tables and BBQ areas at a 649m **lookout** (50min), the highest point reached today. The lane continues downhill in wide curves past another picnic area, soon levelling out over red rock to touch on a surfaced road. Here turn right past a driveway for a house, and onto a lane without crossing the road. Over a rise is a lovely view to Civitella del Lago. At a power line the lane veers left. At a high green netted fence around a **sports ground**, turn right down to the road, then right again along the tarmac back to the shrine junction near the walk start. Go left back past the **cemetery** to return to the village **car park** (1hr).

A good lane leads through farmland in the early part of the walk

WALK 22
Todi and the River Tiber

Start/Finish	Giardino Guglielmo Oberdan, Todi/Pontecuti
Distance	4.3km
Descent	200m
Difficulty	Grade 1
Walking time	1hr
Maps	Parco Fluviale del Tevere 1:25,000 Monte Merli Editrice or free local map Todi 1:15,000 Geoplan
Refreshments	There is a café at Pontecuti.
Public transport	From Pontecuti an afternoon bus (Mon–Sat) can be taken back to Todi Consolazione; from there a short stroll leads back to the Giardino.
Access	On the western edge of Todi, the Giardino Guglielmo Oberdan is also referred to on maps as the Stazione Funivia for the lift down to the Porta Orvietana car park.

The walk begins in the beautiful hill town of Todi at a public garden that doubles as a magnificent belvedere. A straightforward route, it is a nice way to spend a couple of hours walking down to the River Tiber to follow its flow east, as it makes its way towards Rome. Local route Circuito del Paesaggio (landscape circuit) n.6 is followed and has markers in the shape of low wooden poles at strategic forks. The walk conclusion is the old village of Pontecuti, once a fortified settlement at a key river crossing. Afterwards, instead of riding the bus back to Todi, you can retrace your steps – allow 1hr 20min back up the hill to Todi.

Once you have admired the wonderful views from the **Giardino Guglielmo Oberdan** (400m), in lieu of the ride on the lift/funicular, follow the 'Percorso Pedonale Alternativo all'Ascensore'. Beginning in the opposite corner of the gardens to the lift, a ramp passes houses and you are soon pointed left down flights of steps through shady trees dropping below the town walls. At

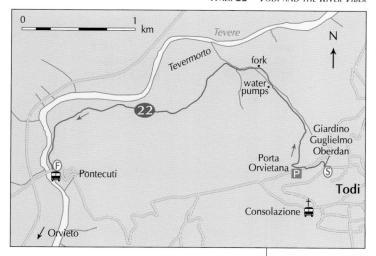

Looking back to Todi

Well-kept fields below Todi

The blocks are reminders of catastrophic landslips in the 1800s caused by blocked underground drainage channels.

a lower path, keep left passing massive collapsed ivy-clad masonry blocks. ◄ It is only minutes to the **Porta Orvietana car park**. Cross to the opposite side where a sign for the 'Circuito del Paesaggio 6' points you through a commemorative arch and into parkland dotted with poplars. Curving right, a lane is soon joined in steady descent. Ignore the next arrow right unless you need the picnic tables, and continue NNW. This will quickly see you out of tree cover to enjoy more vast views of rolling hills, not to mention a glimpse of the Tiber far below.

The route soon begins decisive descent on a rutted track in between fields and alongside a stream. Further down you skirt **water pumps** and continue downhill to reach a wider lane on the valley floor. Here **fork** left (W) through an area known as **Tevermorto**. Rural properties with thriving orchards and olive groves are passed, the narrow road alternating surfaced with gravel sections. Over a rise, you draw closer to the mighty Tiber and curve S on the last leg. A modest old stone portal announces the entrance to **Pontecuti** (205m, 1hr).

In all likelihood, Pontecuti took its name from '**pointed bridge**' for its original arched shape back in the 1200s. The current structure is a post-Second World War reconstruction, and can be appreciated from a friendly riverside café.

WALK 23
Vasciano–Montenero

Start/Finish	Vasciano
Distance	17km
Ascent/Descent	280m/280m
Difficulty	Grade 1–2
Walking time	4hr 30min
Refreshments	Vasciano has a bar-cum-grocery shop while meals may be available at Agriturismo I Rossi before Montenero (tel 075 8947079). To be on the safe side set out with your own supplies. Water is on tap at the villages.
Public transport	Vasciano has the rare (Mon–Sat) bus from Todi, as does Pesciano.
Access	Vasciano is 6km south of Todi. Park on the roadside at the village.

This pleasant walk follows local route 'Circuito del Paesaggio 5', with arrows and markers at junctions throughout. It is essentially a stroll through the peaceful hilly countryside touching on the rural settlement or two. There is a 1hr stretch of surfaced road on the central section of the walk, however, it sees little traffic and is quite scenic. An early afternoon bus can be caught from Bivio Pesciano back to Vasciano if desired, but it would be a pity to miss the curious fortified village of Montenero, a highlight of this walk.

At **Vasciano** (340m) and the Bar-Alimentari on the main road, turn down to the church, where you will find a 'Circuito del Paesaggio 5' pole pointing you left. This quickly leaves the village behind, cutting initially W between fields to join a wider lane. Lovely views back to Todi and over rolling hills dotted with fortified settlements are enjoyed. A group of partly renovated buildings is soon reached – the Ospedaletto was a 12th-century hospital-cum-leprosarium complete with a chapel. You continue mostly S across peaceful meadows and woodland, gradually descending towards the river (Torrente Arnata), which can be heard cascading below. Near

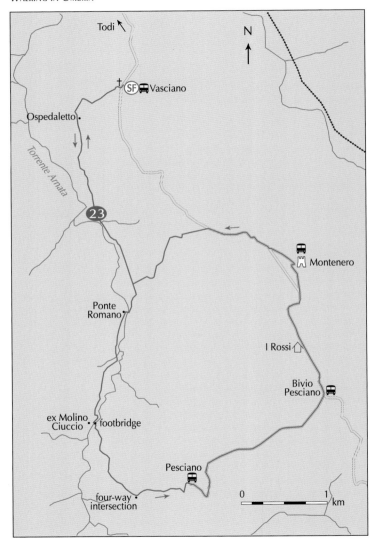

A modest old bridge, the Ponte Romano, is crossed during the walk

a house, a lane lined with cypresses joins from the left (45min) – the return route. But you keep straight ahead (S) to pass an old mill building and on to the so-called **Ponte Romano** (Roman bridge), although it only dates back to the Middle Ages.

Turn right to cross the old arch then branch immediately left following the opposite bank on a clear lane amid lighter Mediterranean scrub. You proceed consistently S, high above Torrente Arnata and over a rise with a ruined building on the edge of a field. Not far on, n.5 leaves the leisurely lane to fork abruptly left as a faint path down to the grounds of **ex Molino Ciuccio** (295m). The former mill is now a private home, and you carefully skirt the lawn to the riverbank and a footbridge. This leads back over the stream to a quiet lane steadily uphill SE through fields and past farms and hillsides bright with rock roses and broom.

At a **four-way intersection** of dirt roads, n.5 turns left, climbing steeply NE for the last leg to **Pesciano** (470m, 1hr 15min). This tiny low-key village doubles as a wonderful belvedere. Near picnic tables, take the minor road downhill, with views to where the castle of Sismano stands out southeast. A windswept ridge leads

NE to **Bivio Pesciano** (bus stop) where you fork left on the SP379 road past **Agriturismo I Rossi** and up a hill to the junction right for **Montenero**, only minutes further on (410m, 1hr).

> A handful of souls – five at the time of writing – still inhabit this **medieval village**, which comprises a huge central stone castle surrounded by a semi-circle of miniature terraced houses. This was originally a complete ring, with entry by way of a drawbridge.

From the bus stop in the village square, take the pine-lined road back out to the main road (SP379) and go right (NW). Soon ignore the signed fork right for 'n.5' and stick to the tarmac through a pine wood to a marked turn-off left (30min). An old lane with remnant stone paving slabs leads SW for the most part gently descending out of the wood but soon accompanied by rows of cypress trees. It reaches the valley floor not far from the river at the fork encountered on the outward stretch (15min). Turn right to return to **Vasciano** (45min).

The marvellous medieval village of Montenero

From Assisi's Rocca Minore looking over to the Rocca Maggiore (Walk 25)

INTRODUCTION

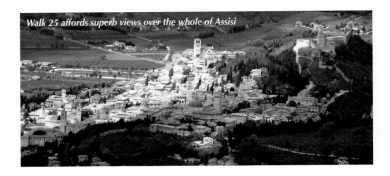

Walk 25 affords superb views over the whole of Assisi

Southeast from the regional capital Perugia stands Bettona, justifiably dubbed 'the balcony of Umbria' for its superb scenic ridge location. The little-visited laidback village is ringed with intact medieval walls of sandstone atop massive stone blocks laid by the ancient Etruscans. The occasional bus from Perugia and Assisi calls in, and Walk 24 starts here. Accommodation is available. A crow's flight away in renowned wine country are the utterly charming towns of Bevagna and Montefalco. Both have buses and accommodation and are linked by Walk 27.

Opposite stands the beautiful landmark town of Assisi. It clings to a steep hillside over the wide Chiascio-Topino river plain where rows of poplars and cypresses separate a vivid green patchwork of cultivated fields and settlements. Trains between Perugia and Foligno pull in at the Santa Maria degli Angeli station, with connecting buses climbing the short distance to the town. Synonymous with Saint Francis, Assisi attracts coach loads of the faithful as well as art lovers to its magnificent Basilica, resplendent once more thanks to restoration in the wake of the 1997 earthquake that shook the region. For walkers, there is neighbouring Monte Subasio, an extensive limestone massif and park area explored in Walk 25. The southeastern reaches are covered in Walk 26, which starts out from delightful Spello. It boasts frescoed masterpieces of Renaissance art, Roman ruins and an ancient aqueduct. The town (Spello Borgo) is more easily reached by bus from neighbouring Foligno or Assisi than train despite the vicinity of the railway.

WALK 24

Bettona–Collemancio

Start/Finish	Piazza Garibaldi, Bettona
Distance	17km
Ascent/Descent	500m/500m
Difficulty	Grade 2–3
Walking time	5hr 10min (4hr from Cinque Cerri)
Maps	Camminare in Umbria 1:50,000 Trasimeno-Medio Tevere, Istituto Geografico Adriatico
Refreshments	Restaurants are found at both Bettona and Collemancio, while Bettona has groceries for picnic needs.
Public transport	Daily buses from Assisi and Perugia serve Bettona.
Access	Piazza Garibaldi is the main village square, easily identified by its café, historic palazzos and Municipio. By car you can drive as far as Cinque Cerri, cutting 1hr 10min off the walk total.

Setting out from the charming hill town of Bettona, this is a rather long but very rewarding walk through wooded hills. It entails a drawn-out descent to the Torrente Sambro, followed by a similarly long ascent to a wonderfully panoramic ridge, that comes to a fitting conclusion at the tiny walled village of Collemancio in a world of its own. The return leg drops to the river again before climbing back up to Bettona.

With the exception of the opening section – tarmac as far as Cinque Cerri (avoidable by driving) – a series of lanes, unsurfaced roads and paths are followed, as is fairly frequent red/white M01 paint waymarking. The only difficulties might be encountered at the Sambro which needs crossing twice: there is no bridge at either point and after rain the stepping stones may be under water so expect to ford. A final possible setback could be the ensuing uphill stretch, which can be overgrown in places.

Leave **Bettona** (442m) from Piazza Garibaldi by walking SE along Corso Marconi–Via XX Settembre and out the Etruscan medieval walls. Continue straight ahead to the intersection then go left and first right on Via Belvedere signed for route 'M01'. This heads decidedly uphill

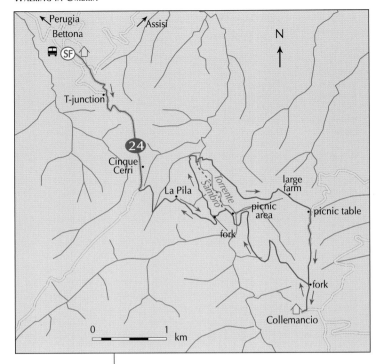

passing houses, with lovely views back to Bettona and the Chiascio plain. At a **T-junction** you go left (S) on the SP402 along a scenic crest, finally dipping to picnic tables at the defunct eatery at **Cinque Cerri** (five oaks) (434m, 35min).

A matter of metres on, M01 finally leaves the surfaced road to take a lane up to a junction where you take the turn-off for La Pila. A shady track leads to the farm itself, **La Pila**. Here ignore the two tracks off to the right, and take the rough stony track that drops SE below a ruined building, heading into woodland where it narrows. The path bears left (NW) passing a marked **fork** (the return route) and gently sloping down to the unsurfaced

Wading across the Sambro

road on the valley floor. Go right and very soon turn off left to cross the **Torrente Sambro** (272m). ▶

A path SE takes over, climbing steadily through wood, overgrown at times. After a field of olive trees, a lane is joined heading E and up to a **large farm** (Azienda Santa Lucia) in a panoramic position. Keep right as per waymarks through to a shady **picnic table** on the roadside with a brilliant view to Assisi and Monte Subasio northeast, the Apennines beyond. Turn right (S) up the road past a batch of houses, to where a scenic ridge lane proceeds through fields to the signed **fork** (2hr 10min) for the return route. A short stroll away is the unmissable delightful walled village of **Collemancio** (407m, 10min return). Public transport once served the village, but the bus stop has been unofficially converted into a shrine, complete with a chair for meditative waits.

Return to the fork and branch downhill NW on a lane past a farm and winding through patches of fire-blackened shrub vegetation. This concludes with the second crossing of **Torrente Sambro**. Turn right along the unsurfaced road to a nearby **picnic area** (272m, 50min).

The Sambro may need fording.

The inviting entrance to Collemancio

Alternative route

From the picnic area you can continue along the unsurfaced road past a house to pick up the path followed on the outward stretch. At least 20min extra needs to be allowed.

Here a marked narrow path branches left for a rather steep short cut up to the marked fork where the outward route is joined (15min). Then go left to retrace your steps via **La Pila** and **Cinque Cerri** and finally back to **Bettona** (442m, 1hr 10min).

WALK 25
Monte Subasio

Start/Finish	Piazza Matteotti, Assisi
Distance	14.3km; or 12.2km
Ascent/Descent	800m/800m; or 650m/650m
Difficulty	Grade 2–3
Walking time	5hr; or 4hr (plus 30min for Eremo delle Carceri visit)
Maps	Parco del Monte Subasio 1:25,000 Monte Merli Editrice
Refreshments	Take drinking water and a picnic; the only facility is a snack bar near Eremo delle Carceri
Public transport	Local buses from Santa Maria degli Angeli railway station terminate at Piazza Matteotti.
Access	Piazza Matteotti and its car park are located on the upper northeastern side of Assisi.

This full day's walk is long but very worthwhile (and a short cut is possible). It commences at the beautiful town of Assisi and explores Monte Subasio, the vast brooding limestone mountain that forms its backdrop. Recognisable from afar for its summital bald patch, like a monk's tonsure, it is an unparalleled lookout over the Chiascio-Topino river plain, making for grandiose vistas on a clear day. In summertime the mountain's uppermost meadows are a riot of white narcissus and orchids, while overhead are birds of prey such as the goshawk and buzzard.

Go equipped with sun protection and warm weatherproof gear as Subasio has quite a reputation for wind – it's no coincidence that local paragliding groups use the flat summit as a launch site.

As early as the 1400s Monte Subasio was **communal property**; in return for grazing rights and firewood the townsfolk had the responsibility of safeguarding the wood, including the ancient holm oaks that enclose the Eremo delle Carceri hermitage, a highlight of this walk. These days the mountain is a protected regional park.

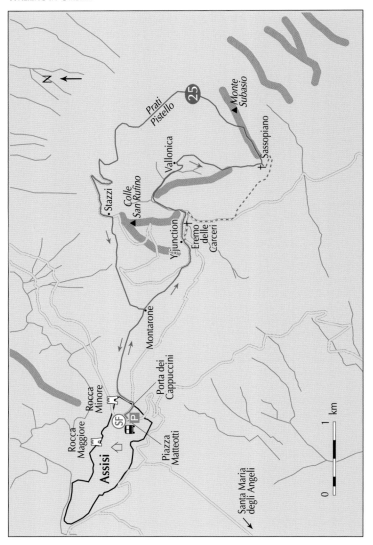

WALK 25 – MONTE SUBASIO

From **Piazza Matteotti** (460m) turn up Via Eremo delle Carceri as far as the **Porta dei Cappuccini** and exit through the 14th-century town walls. Immediately outside fork left up the lane lined with cypress trees and marked red/white n.50. It soon reaches the tower of **Rocca Minore** where a lovely view can be enjoyed over to the impressive Rocca Maggiore fortress. Go right (E) in common with the blue/yellow pilgrim route to Rome for a steady relentless climb through woodland, with the occasional glimpse to the plain below. You pass the **Montarone** (797m) fork where the return route slots in, and now the path levels out somewhat. On reaching the road, fork right and follow it downhill to the **Y-junction**. Turn right for the short stroll to the atmospheric **Eremo delle Carceri** (820m, 1hr); take the left turn and follow n.50 to miss out the detour.

> **St Francis** spent long periods in meditation here. Visitors can squeeze through the narrow passageways and monks' cells, and admire a gnarled and battered holm oak tree where the holy man conversed with the birds.

Eremo delle Carceri hidden away in the woods

123

After following the quiet road (the SP251 for San Benedetto) E, curving above the hermitage, at a bend, branch off left (N) on path n.50, parting way with the tarmac and the pilgrims. This follows the Fosso delle Carceri gully. According to legend only runs with water when Assisi is threatened with catastrophe! It is a steady and possibly slippery climb through damp wood, the trees draped with ivy and moss. Further up it veers right (SE) up past banks of rose bushes and lavendar planted for experimental purposes, to come out above the treeline at the beginning of the bare pasture spreading up to the top of Monte Subasio.

At signed junction **Vallonica** (1059m, 1hr) go right along the rough lane past the forestry commission hut Rifugio Vallonica. Continue S past grazing horses and melodious skylarks to the superb lookout and wooden cross of **Sassopiano** (1124m, 20min). The perfect place for a memorable scenic picnic, it offers spectacular views to Perugia, Assisi and Lago Trasimeno. The shorter variant branches off here.

Short cut via Eremo delle Carceri
Fork downhill on signed path 'n.60' in rapid descent NW into woodland. It joins the surfaced road to cross Fosso delle Carceri and back to Eremo delle Carceri. Retrace the outward paths back to Assisi (50min).

Go NE across the grassy slopes – no actual path – heading for the windsock and fence at a paragliding launch point (1270m, 20min). ◄ Here go left on the red gravel road over bare terrain with ever-changing views to the rugged peaks of the Apennine chain north-northeast, snowcapped well into spring. Northwest are Monte Tezio and Acuto in the Upper Tiber Valley.

After crossing Prati Pistello the road drops gradually in wide curves to a picnic area **Stazzi** (1083m, 1hr). Curving towards the knoll Colle San Rufino, n.53 breaks off as a path, descending due W over grassy terrain dotted with juniper bushes alongside dark conifer plantation.

Not much further east is the actual 1290m top of Monte Subasio studded with aerials.

Soon back in woodland a clear track continues downhill – follow waymarking faithfully at the many forks. After passing a mechanical contraption rusting in a clearing, you proceed to the **Montarone** (797m) junction encountered early on. Go right here to return to Piazza Matteotti and **Assisi** (1hr 20min).

Sassopiano is a great belvedere

WALK 26
Spello and Monte Pietrolungo

Start/Finish	Fonte della Bulgarella, Spello
Distance	12.3km
Ascent/Descent	600m/600m
Difficulty	Grade 2
Walking time	3hr 45min
Maps	Parco del Monte Subasio 1:25,000 Monte Merli Editrice
Refreshments	Collepino has a café and restaurant, while Spello has shops for picnic food.
Access	Fonte della Bulgarella, a natural spring with taps, is on the northern uppermost edge of Spello. It is located not far from Porta Montanara on the road for Collepino. On foot from the town it takes 10min.

Passing through a quiet farming valley, a fascinating stretch of Roman aqueduct is followed in the opening part of this walk. Recently cleaned up and equipped with information points in both English and Italian, it makes for a memorable stroll from the back door of Spello, an easy Grade 1 route as far as the fountain below Collepino (allow 2hr 30min total returning the same way). However, the complete loop described here makes for a great day exploring the southeastern flanks of Monte Subasio and its park, including wide-sweeping views. Afterwards allow plenty of time to wander around delightful Spello.

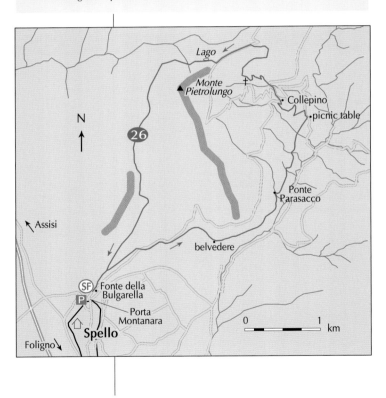

Fonte della Bulgarella where the walk begins

Before setting out from **Fonte della Bulgarella** (310m), fill up your drinking bottle with the deliciously cool water. Then fork uphill following the well-signed route for the 'Acquedotto romano', also red/white n.52, soon branching right (NE) to separate from n.50, the return way. Flanking the old stone wall of the aqueduct, the route passes between well-tended olive groves bright with red poppies in spring, and has numerous points of interests marked by signs, as well as openings to show the interior water channel.

Constructed in the Augustan era, the **aqueduct** functioned up to the Middle Ages when it fell into disuse through lack of maintenance, but was refurbished in the 1700s, supplying over 50 cisterns and fountains in its heyday. Remarkably, it was operational until the early 1900s.

The road is crossed and a **belvedere** reached where Spello can be admired from a comfortable innovative bench. Soon the path dips underneath the wall and spirals back up to bear N into a side valley and cross **Ponte Parasacco**, a built-up wall-cum-bridge, before coming to

127

The Aqueduct route accompanied by poppies and olive trees.

For the short version of this walk, turn back here and retrace your steps to Fonte della Bulgarella.

log benches. From here on the only evidence of the aqueduct are two bridges as the way begins climbing with glimpses of the village high above. Past rural properties you will emerge on the roadside and a **picnic table** (1hr 15min, 455m). ◄

Turn uphill on the road for a matter of metres to where the path resumes left steeply – follow red/white waymarks carefully at forks. After curving W, you emerge at **Collepino** (600m, 15min). A tiny hamlet, it boasts a café and restaurant.

Take the road uphill, keeping right for San Giovanni and n.52. At the first bend, a clear path forks left (NW) straight up into woodland. At a lane and Fontana San Silvestro go right to pass a Romanesque chapel belonging to an abbey founded here by St Benedict in 523. The resumption of the path NE uphill soon means wonderful views east towards the rugged Apennines, snowcapped well into spring. After a hut the gradient eases as you head W to join a road (900m, 1hr). Here turn left in descent to the signed turn-off **Lago** (845m) where you need to go right on n.56. A good track through a conifer plantation,

The descent enjoys a lovely outlook

it passes a diminutive lake in a shallow depression, or dolina, caused by water eroding the limestone beneath. After a picnic table ignore the turn-off right for n.56 and keep left on the unmarked lane as it heads W below Monte Pietrolungo and abandoned stone terracing. ▸

You join forces with n.50 on a clear wide lane leading S through a picnic area in common with a yellow/blue pilgrim route before emerging from the cover of trees to enjoy wide-reaching views across the vast cultivated plain of the Topino River and down to Spello. Fields planted with olives accompany you to the walk conclusion down at **Fonte della Bulgarella** (1hr 15min).

Gaps in the trees mean glimpses northwest to the landmark dome of S Maria degli Angeli below Assisi.

WALK 27
Bevagna to Montefalco

Start/Finish	Piazza Silvestri, Bevagna/Piazza del Comune, Montefalco
Distance	13km
Ascent/Descent	400m/150m
Difficulty	Grade 1–2
Walking time	3hr 30min
Maps	Camminare in Umbria 1:50,000 Trasimeno-Medio Tevere, Istituto Geografico Adriatico
Refreshments	Both villages have grocery shops, cafés and restaurants. En route snacks may be available if the Pian di Boccio camping ground is open (tel 0742 360391).
Public transport	To return to Bevagna from Montefalco there is a handy afternoon bus (Mon–Sat). Otherwise do it by taxi (tel 380 8064447, www.leviedellumbria.it).
Access	The piazzas are the principal squares in the two villages and are centrally located thus easy to find.

This is a very lovely walk through the rolling cultivated hills of central Umbria where the landscape is dominated by olive groves and vineyards responsible for producing the district's famed red wines – notably Rosso di Montefalco and Sagrantino. Additional interest comes by way of two charming walled towns. Quiet Bevagna was a Roman settlement, and remnants of ancient baths and mosaics are visible in the surviving medieval layout. Better known Montefalco occupies an elevated position; from its centrally located piazza, a glance down any alley is met with fine views over the countryside.

There is no waymarking at all en route so follow the directions to the letter. Moreover, there are quite lengthy stretches of tarmac at the walk start and in the middle. Do not let these minor points put you off!

From **Piazza Silvestri** in Bevagna (208m) walk SW along paved Corso Amendola lined with old houses, and exit the town walls through Porta Sant'Agostino. Turn left on Via San Salvatore and soon over two bridges in quick succession. Continue straight ahead on Via Sant'Antonio amid grape vines, olive groves and walnut trees, climbing

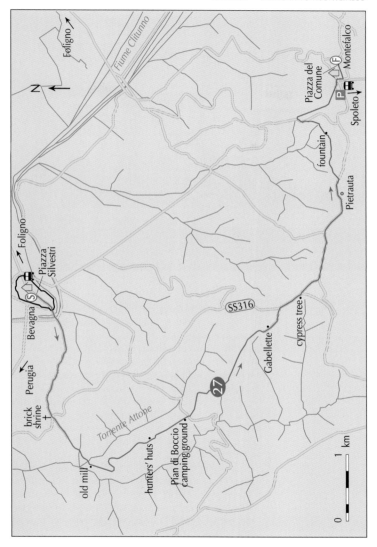

Bevagna's Piazza Silvestri

past properties. A curve right reveals sweeping views over the valley to Assisi and Spello backed by Monte Subasio.

Up at a four-way intersection with a **brick shrine** (Madonna delle Quattro Chiavi) keep straight ahead (sign for 'Agriturismo Il Rotolone') and down the other side. This heads into the Attone Valley, past oak trees that are home to multitudes of twittering birds. At the bottom of the hill the road gives way to a lane, curving left along the edge of a field to poplar trees and a ruined **old mill** (Molino dell'Attone 220m, 45min) all but concealed by thriving undergrowth. Just before the building branch left (SSW) onto a muddy tractor track that climbs towards woodland.

Once in the trees it curves uphill (ignoring a turn-off right) with a couple of changes of direction. At a field the way narrows to a rather overgrown path (although a track continues in parallel on the left) but it is not far to where a wider clay-based lane re-appears to lead over a rise to **hunters' huts** and an olive plantation.

Not far along you join an unsurfaced road with lamp posts; this leads through the **Pian di Boccio camping ground** (321m, 45min). Exit the premises past the café-reception building and walk out to the road (SP443). Opposite, take unsurfaced Via Colcimino, a gentle uphill through an olive grove to a beautiful panoramic ridge where most of Umbria seems visible, with mountainous ridges over cultivated plains and picturesque settlements. Keep on past the houses and a shrine to a gentle descent ESE through vineyards edged with roses – now looking ahead to Montefalco perched on its ridge. At a rise (and road sign for 'Via Colcimino dal 7 al 9' to the right) the surfaced road veers left but you continue in the same direction on a clear lane.

This climbs and curves in a dog leg past a farm and left onto a quiet tarmac road that traverses the hamlet of **Gabellette**, although no sign tells you so. Out at the main road SS316, fork right – watching out for traffic – to a cluster of houses. As you reach a prominent **cypress tree**

Looking across to Monte Subasio

133

on the right-hand side of the road, turn left for a minor road over a rise to join the SP445. Go left (E) to traverse the strung-out settlement of **Pietrauta** (397m). While this stretch of road is rather long, there are good views as it follows a ridge.

A matter of metres after the village bar, at a sign for 'B&B La Cardoncina', leave the tarmac for a rough stony lane on the left that drops NE following a power line at first. Peaceful and rural, it passes sheds and a house then a **fountain** dated 1898. Soon afterwards you emerge on the SP444 opposite a villa. Turn left for the short distance to a curve (before the petrol station) then sharp right past a shrine and straight ahead on a lovely lane SSE Via del Verziere. Your destination, inviting **Montefalco**, is close at hand now spread over its crest-knoll ahead. The gentle climb concludes at a car park alongside Hotel Villa Pambuffetti where you keep left up to the corner of the town walls.

A short distance away to the right is graceful Porta di Sant'Agostino and its clock. This lets you into the beautiful town centre and Corso Goffredo Mameli, lined with enticing shops and wine bars where the local delicacies can be tasted. Up the top is the walk conclusion, **Piazza del Comune** of Montefalco (472m, 2hr).

5 SPOLETO AND THE VALNERINA

The path climbs to I Camini on Monteluco (Walk 28)

INTRODUCTION

The bare slopes of Monte Coscerno make for pleasant walking (Walk 32)

In 1896 the great German writer JW von Goethe paid an inspiring visit to Umbria: 'I climbed up to Spoleto and was on the aqueduct, which also serves as a bridge between two mountains. The ten arches of brickwork have stood there so calmly during the centuries, and water still gushes forth everywhere in Spoleto.'

Thankfully, little has changed since his visit including the superb 13th-century Ponte delle Torri, crossed in Walks 28 and 29. A fascinating 14th-century Rocca fortress and magnificent frescoed Duomo also feature on the long list of highlights. With plenty of accommodation and shops, Spoleto is a fine base for exploring the district. It is well served

by public transport; trains pull in at the foot of the hill and city buses cover the remaining distance. For something completely different, Walk 30 follows the route of the long-abandoned railway line that loops through surprisingly rugged landscapes on its wonderful way to Norcia.

The railway spends many a kilometre in Valnerina, a renowned river valley whose cliff edges are dotted with Romanesque churches and photogenic villages; all offer accommodation and bus services. Erstwhile medieval fortress Vallo di Nera is a gem, perfectly restored, and the start of Walk 31. Castel San Felice is a veritable island on the valley floor with a delightful old abbey and

Walk 29 gives you the chance to admire Spoleto's Rocca

monastery, converted into a modest hotel. Scheggino, on the other hand, is a triangular medieval fortified settlement. Many houses were built on the river level, but they now stand behind a sturdy wall to protect them from flooding; a plaque in the main square shows the astounding height the water reached in 1936. Dominating central Valnerina is Monte Coscerno, a vast elongated mountain accessible from Gavillo on Walk 32.

A short drive eastwards on tortuous panoramic roads – or a bus trip via Serravalle and the Nera valley floor – leads to Cascia in a world of its own in a high valley. It is a remarkable magnet for visitors who flock from all over the world to pay homage to local girl and miracle weaver Saint Rita.

For walkers, Cascia has great routes to offer (Walks 33 and 34). The village's home-style cuisine benefits from delicate saffron that grows locally. Accommodation, restaurants, shops and indescribable souvenirs are abundant.

WALK 28
Spoleto and Monteluco

Start/Finish	Piazza del Duomo, Spoleto
Distance	10.5km
Ascent/Descent	550m/550m
Difficulty	Grade 1–2
Walking time	3hr 45min
Maps	Spoleto city map and Monti di Spoleto e della Media Valnerina 1:25,000 SER
Refreshments	There are several café-restaurants on Monteluco, but many close on weekdays off-season so carry a picnic from Spoleto to be sure.
Access	Piazza del Duomo is located in the upper part of Spoleto and is easily reached on foot. Alternatively take the *percorso meccanizzato* (escalator) that begins on the lower northwest edge of town near Via della Ponzianina; at the top you exit just below the Rocca – turn left along pedestrian Via Gattaponi to pick up the walk.

This is a beautiful circuit starting out from magnificent Spoleto via the memorable 13th-century Ponte delle Torri, at 80m high and 230m long, reputedly Europe's highest ancient stone bridge, once an aqueduct. The route climbs to Monteluco. Farmland and woods are traversed on mostly limestone terrain. Evergreen Mediterranean oaks dominate vegetation, along with flowers such as cyclamens, tree heather and aromatic bushes. Red/white waymarking is clear and frequent at first, although rather scarce later on so follow instructions carefully. A torch is handy for the short tunnel.

Currently closed, Ponte delle Torri will hopefully re-open in 2019. Slot into the walk at San Pietro (a short distance outside the walls) for the time being.

From **Piazza del Duomo** (395m) go up the wide stepped way, Via dell'Arringo. At the top turn left on Via Aurelio Saffi and go under its arches. Keep straight on through a small square and up to a corner of the grandiose **Rocca** premises. Take the narrow road Via del Ponte flanking the walls, past a panoramic café and hotel to the famous **Ponte delle Torri**. ◄ Cross this amazing bridge and at the end keep right to a fountain and signposts (411m). Here it is left on n.1, an old winding stepped way past a tower

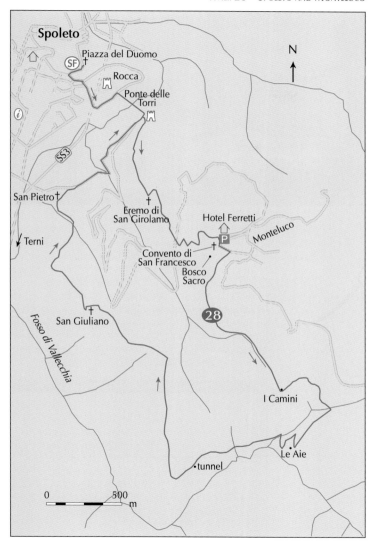

Spoleto

Piazza del Duomo

SF

Rocca

Ponte delle Torri

SS3

San Pietro

Eremo di San Girolamo

Hotel Ferretti

P

Monteluco

Terni

Convento di San Francesco

Bosco Sacro

28

San Giuliano

Fosso di Vallecchia

I Camini

Le Aie

tunnel

N

0   500   m

Piazza del Duomo is a beautiful place to start

(Fortilizo dei Mulini) heading into woodland with great views over the Rocca and bridge with its topmost water channel. Soon ignore the left turn-off for the Giro dei Condotti (Walk 29) and continue essentially SSE, zigzagging upwards in common with blue/yellow markings of the Via Francigena. Further up you touch on the former **Eremo di San Girolamo** (600m), then it is not far up to where the SP462 road is crossed. The path resumes up to a cross before flanking the perimeter walls of an old monastery and chapel. You head through to Albergo Ferretti and a **car park on Monteluco** (768m, 1hr 10min).

THE MOUNT OF MONTELUCO

Flanking the town of Spoleto is the modest wooded mount of Monteluco. The name derives from 'lucus', an ancient Roman 'holy wood' dedicated to Jove. And as of the fifth century, the place attracted veritable hosts of hermits. The first to venture onto the mount and set up in isolation was St Isaac, fleeing persecution in Syria, and later arrivals included St Francis in the 1100s. These days, picnickers and walkers come for the woods and pathways.

Turn right (n.1) on the road past picnic tables and the entrance to the **Convento di San Francesco** aka Santuario di Monteluco. Close-by is the gate for the **Bosco Sacro** ('holy wood'), worth an exploratory wander, time permitting. Stay on the road as it crosses park ground, but branch first right for an unsurfaced road at a hotel amid chestnut trees. Mostly S-SSE, you pass houses and the way narrows to a path in gentle ascent through a conifer plantation to the picnic/BBQ area **I Camini** (880m). ▶ Fork right downhill on a wide lane lined with broom bushes, with spaces affording lovely views over the wooded hills.

Here you part ways with the Via Francigena, which climbs off left (N).

Further down, at a T-junction above buildings, keep right downhill. After the next bend as you approach the farm (**Le Aie**), fork right off the lane at the first opportunity. Devoid of waymarking due to rerouting to avoid the farm premises, this passes a shed and drops steeply into the valley. Once over the dry stream bed keep immediately left in the warren of paths and in a matter of minutes you'll reach the signpost for 'Le Aie' (762m, 50min) where n.1 reappears.

A lovely sun-blessed path now coasts SW through masses of Mediterranean flowers and herbs. Traces are visible of an old paved way constructed to accompany a minor aqueduct through a short (60m long) tunnel dating back to 1856 – walk straight through. ▶

A torch is handy but not essential.

Afterwards the path bears right (N). Beautiful views open up over the Vallecchia Valley hemmed in by wooded hills, while the San Giuliano monastic complex soon comes into view ahead, high over the cultivated plain adjacent Spoleto. At a T-junction with a rough track, you plunge left (NW) – watch your step on the loose stones. Things become gentler at **San Giuliano** (628m, 40min), a combination of Romanesque church and restaurant with a gorgeous lookout over the Rocca and town. This is believed to be the site of the early hermitage founded by St Isaac, and the great Michelangelo reportedly sojourned here during the Renaissance.

In front of the buildings follow the sign for the dirt track down along the edge of a field and into the wood onto another loose rock path. This concludes at a minor

Duck your head and breathe in before entering the short tunnel!

road and camping ground, where you turn right for the graceful church of **San Pietro** dating back to the fifth century (390m, 30min). The SP462 road is not far away – follow it straight ahead (NE) to return to **Ponte delle Torri** (20min) and retrace your steps back to **Piazza del Duomo** (15min).

WALK 29
Giro dei Condotti

Start/Finish	Piazza del Duomo, Spoleto
Distance	5.2km; or 8.2km
Ascent/Descent	60m; or 450m
Difficulty	Grade 1; or Grade 1–2
Walking time	1hr 20min; or 3hr
Maps	Spoleto city map and Monti di Spoleto e della Media Valnerina 1:25,000 SER
Refreshments	Take your own as there is nothing en route.
Access	See Walk 28 for details.

A must-do memorable stroll with superb views that takes in three of Spoleto's top sights – the magnificent Romanesque Duomo, the 14th-century Rocca and the renowned 13th-century Ponte delle Torri bridge-cum-aqueduct (80m high and 230m long). After leaving town, the 'Giro dei Condotti' ('aqueduct tour') goes through lovely woodland, looping via San Ponziano before climbing back to the piazza via a steep stairway. In 2006 the Spoleto Comune saw fit to restore the route, to the delight of walkers and runners.

Due to the brevity of the walk, an optional extension is given – this follows the wooded cleft of Valcieca, before returning on high tracks that look out over the cultivated plains to rejoin the main route close to Ponte Sanguineto.

Leave **Piazza del Duomo** (395m) on the wide stepped way Via dell'Arringo. At the top turn left on Via Aurelio Saffi, under its arches and through a small square. Up at a corner of the grandiose **Rocca** premises, take the narrow road Via del Ponte flanking the walls, past a panoramic café and hotel to the famous **Ponte delle Torri**. ▶ Cross the marvellous bridge and, at the end, keep right to a fountain and signposts (411m, 15min). You soon find yourself going left climbing on an old winding stepped way past a tower (Fortilizo dei Mulini) heading into wood. Not far up the Giro dei Condotti forks left (NE) parting ways with the Monteluco route (Walk 28). The path cuts

Ponte delle Torri is currently closed. By all means do the route in reverse as far as Ponte Sanguineto and access the extension.

Crossing marvellous Ponte delle Torri

through woodland with numerous Mediterranean species, pretty cyclamens and rock roses and contines along the base of Monteluco with a beautiful outlook to the bridge and Rocca, enjoyable from any of the well placed benches. Around a corner, a sign points left for a short cut via ruined church of S Elisabetta and straight back to Spoleto, but keep on below the sheer line of cliffs SE to **Ponte Sanguineto** (444m, 30min).

Extension

Stay on n.3 in cool shady wood SE up Valcieca, accompanied by traces of an old aqueduct. Ignore the turn-off for 'S Antonio/Monteluco'. Further on the gradient steepens as you bear S and after leaving a lane (which forks off uphill left), the way narrows with plants and branches occasionally attempting to encroach. There is a fleeting glimpse of the **Fosso di Valcieca** chasm then you cross to the left side of the valley for a steeper section. After passing a barbed wire fence you reach a **clearing** with two signposts (797m, 1hr 10min).

At this point you part ways with n.3 and fork left onto an unmarked but clear path, which soon goes downhill

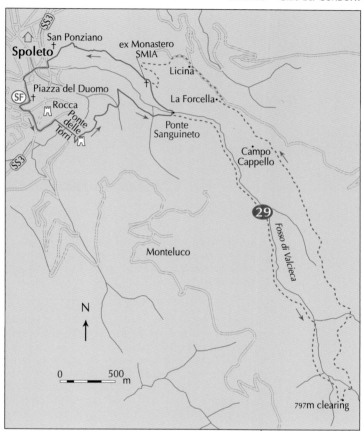

on a gravel base to cross a stream bed. Heading N now it levels out and widens. Downhill through partially cleared woodland and up over a rise it passes through a clearing with a water trough and keeps straight on. After a panoramic stretch, it is downhill past the entrance to **Campo Cappello**, where a white gravel road takes over NW. At houses (**La Forcella**, 578m) fork right then left

The path through olive groves

onto the tarmac (SP463). In common with CAI n.8, you soon keep left at a fork (**Licina**, 570m). Past houses you are pointed left on a dirt track alongside olive groves, which then winds down to the beautifully restored **ex Monastero Santa Maria Inter Angelos** (437m, 1hr) to pick up the main route.

Cross the bridge for the clear path leading NW through olive groves to the beautifully restored **ex Monastero Santa Maria Inter Angelos** (437m) where the extension slots backs in. The signed path continues alongside the buildings for a lovely level scenic track. There are concreted stretches as it descends W and flanks the sprawling **San Ponziano** monastery. At the main road (SS3) it veers left and soon right below the flyover, then on Via Tiro a Segno to a bridge leading back into Spoleto. As you enter the walls there is the option of a leisurely finish – namely the *percorso meccanizzato* (escalator) all the way back up to the Rocca level. But purists will continue straight ahead on foot up Via Ponzianina. A short way up take the first left, Via delle Mura Ciclopiche, a stepped and remarkably steep way along the ancient Roman walls, massive remnants of which can be admired embedded in houses. The fitting conclusion is **Piazza del Duomo** (395m, 35min).

WALK 30
Spoleto to Sant'Anatolia di Narco

Start/Finish	Piazza della Vittoria, Spoleto/bus stop, Sant'Anatolia di Narco
Distance	22km
Ascent/Descent	315m/345m
Difficulty	Grade 1–2
Walking time	5hr 15min
Maps	Spoleto city map and Monti di Spoleto e della Media Valnerina 1:25,000 SER
Refreshments	Go equipped with food and drink as there are no facilities until Sant'Anatolia.
Public transport	Sant'Anatolia di Narco has buses back to Spoleto, otherwise call the shuttle taxi (tel 347 9107977).
Access	Piazza della Vittoria, the 'gateway' to Spoleto, is located on the lower northern edge of town, a 10min walk or short bus ride from the railway station.
Note	There is no artificial lighting at all in the tunnels so a good torch with new batteries is essential. Also, at the time of writing, maintenance work was ongoing so check with the Spoleto Tourist Information Office before setting out.

The fascinating initial 19km stretch of the abandoned Spoleto–Norcia railway is described here, reaching Sant'Anatolia di Narco in Valnerina. An extremely rewarding full-day traverse with gentle gradients, it begins in farmland and woods and short tunnels, before crossing to beautiful Valnerina. The original way runs through the 2km Caprareccia tunnel but as this is closed for the time being you detour via quiet roads before slotting back in for a spectacular descent by way of scenic bridges and a sequence of tunnels both helicoidal and normal. Some red/white waymarking accompanies the track, but it's virtually impossible to go the wrong way. The occasional kilometre 'milestones' still stand alongside. A memorable adventure.

From Spoleto's **Piazza della Vittoria** (310m) cross **Ponte Garibaldi** and take Via Nursina right (NE). Where this intersects Via delle Lettere at a car park, cross over and take the **pedestrian underpass** beneath the main road

147

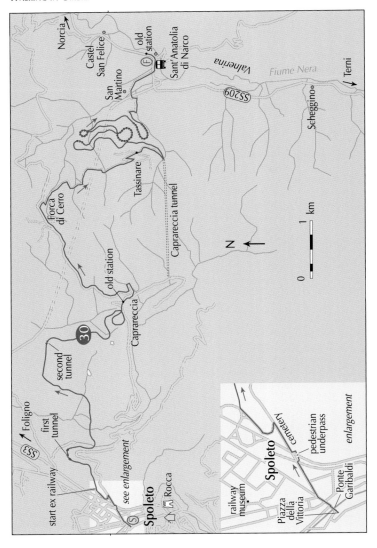

The old railway line looks over Valnerina

towards the **cemetery**. A short way uphill, turn left onto a road – watching out for traffic. Follow this downhill

A MASTERPIECE

Well deserving of the accolade 'masterpiece of railway engineering', the 52km Spoleto–Norcia railway line was inaugurated in 1926, after 13 years under construction slowed by the events of the First World War, as well as the ground-breaking switch from steam power to electricity. No ordinary project, it was first conceived in 1897 and in fact the trains were pre-dated by a steam-powered 'pirobus' service. The design of the narrow gauge railway was entrusted to a Swiss engineer in view of the mountainous terrain, which necessitated multiple bridges and tunnels circling and bending back on themselves. Sadly, services were terminated in 1968, but thankfully much of it is now open to walkers and cyclists. Nowadays the old Spoleto station is a museum housing a model of the railway layout while that of Sant'Anatolia has been converted into an Info Point and marvellous local restaurant.

An arched viaduct carries the track over wooded valleys

around a curve and keep straight ahead at the nearby intersection as per signs for 'Perugia'. Only a couple of metres on, fork right (ENE) onto a lane, which is the start of the **former railway** (15min).

As you head off into woodland, traffic and city sounds fade away quickly, replaced by bird song. It is gentle going uphill through cuttings and across built-up sections to the short **first tunnel** that leads onto a high bridge. A **second tunnel** and bridge are not far on, with vast views across the countryside beyond Eggi, and north to Trevi. Further along, after a long stretch S alongside a fence you walk under a road bridge before a wide circle that gains more height. A bridge leads high over a road and farms to the old station at Caprareccia (597m, 1hr 45min). ◄ Turn up to join the road which climbs in curves NE to the pass **Forca di Cerro** (733m). Not far long a minor road forks R (SSE) down the hillside to the isolated hamlet of **Tassinare**

Here you leave the railway temporarily as the nearby tunnel is closed.

(672m, 1hr 30min). Continue on the lane mostly S to the exit of the Caprareccia tunnel.

In a helicoidal tunnel

Turn L as the track proceeds NNE in gentle descent with wonderful vistas over the rolling hills dotted with farms of Valnerina and the villages of Vallo di Nera, Castel San Felice and Sant'Anatolia. Long loops in the track mean more bridges and a sequence of helicoidal and shorter tunnels. One memorable stretch sees an overhead bridge directly superimposed over a tunnel. The very last tunnel (at km17) is closed so you turn off R for a signed 1.5km way that cuts below San Martino and the across the main road that emerges from its tunnel. A final stretch S brings you to a junction where it's L along the SS209 for the bus stop and old station of **Sant'Anatolia di Narco** (290m, 1hr 45min).

WALK 31
Valnerina

Start/Finish	Bus stop Vallo di Nera/bus stop Scheggino
Distance	8.6km
Ascent/Descent	70m/245m
Difficulty	Grade 1
Walking time	2hr 15min
Maps	Monti di Spoleto e della Media Valnerina 1:25,000 SER
Refreshments	All the villages have cafés and restaurants, and Sant'Anatolia and Scheggino also have groceries.
Public transport	The valley has frequent bus runs so it is easy to return to the start. Not all the buses make the climb to Vallo di Nera, see walk description below for directions to the village on foot. At Scheggino, the bus stop is on the main road.
Access	Vallo di Nera is a short drive off the SS209 along Valnerina. On foot from the bus stop on the main road allow 30min to the village.

This enchanting, easy walk in lovely Valnerina drops in on a string of four beautiful villages: Vallo di Nera, Castel San Felice, Sant'Anatolia di Narco and Scheggino. Built in characteristic age-old pale stone masonry with terracotta roof tiles, they occupy photogenic positions on wooded hillsides or the valley floor where the charming Nera River flows amid willows, poplar trees and old bridges. Do allow extra time for an exploratory wander through each village.

On the walk itself waymarking is fairly constant throughout – but, as usual, follow the directions carefully. As far as Sant'Anatolia the 'Strada degli Eremiti' (Hermits' Way) is followed.

Directions from the bus stop on the main road
Take the road for Vallo di Nera and cross the river. Soon after the first bend a path with a handrail (the old mule track) branches off left to climb through woodland, emerging on the road on the lower edge of the village. Here either go straight ahead on steps or fork left up the tarmac to the bus stop.

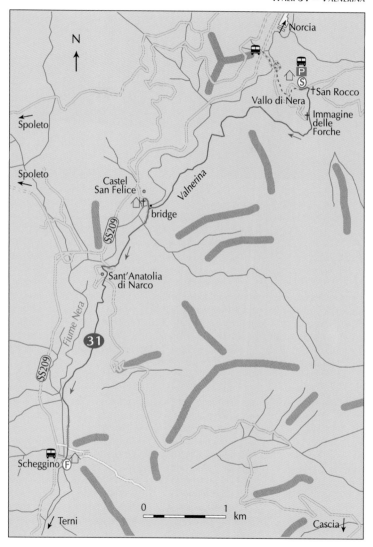

N

Norcia

Spoleto

Spoleto

San Rocco

Vallo di Nera

Immagine delle Forche

Castel San Felice

Valnerina

bridge

SS209

Sant'Anatolia di Narco

Fiume Nera

31

SS209

Scheggino

F

Terni

Cascia

0   1

km

153

The old fortified village of Vallo di Nera

Amid poplar trees on the opposite bank stand the church and monastery (and restaurant) of Abbazia Santi Felice e Mauro, while the peaceful walled village is a short stroll away.

From the bus stop at **Vallo di Nera** (460m) follow CAI route n.12 away from the village then for two successive right turns to the *lavatoio* (wash troughs) and covered portico of the tiny church of **San Rocco**. Then it is immediately sharp left down a paved lane leading S alongside vegetable gardens and stables and into the cover of trees. Accompanied by masses of wild mint, it reaches the 15th-century chapel, **Immagine delle Forche**, with surprisingly vivid frescoes still visible inside. Downhill you cut across a lane then coast W with lovely views back to Vallo di Nera. Guided by red/white markings on trees the way bears SW in gentle descent to the Fiume Nera and the graceful old **bridge** for **Castel San Felice** (290m, 1hr). ◄

Resume the way on the left (eastern) bank of the river on a quiet road, soon unsurfaced. A tree nursery and a derelict chapel are touched on, as you proceed S through fields of maize and vegetable gardens. Immediately after a fountain you cross over the road at the foot of the village of Sant'Anatolia. Follow the lane that curves uphill to re-cross the road and take Via Giacomo Matteotti to Piazza Corrado in **Sant'Anatolia di Narco** (300m, 15min).

Continue on to cross the SP471 road near the Post Office for Via Aldo Moro. Where this ends near ex Convento Santa Croce, go left then immediately right through a recently constructed residential area. A lane S takes over into woodland once more. Not far on at a fork, as the way bears left uphill, leave it for the unmarked track right (SW) that begins to descend. This leads to a lovely path with a timber railing in descent to the valley floor, where a road is joined at a bench under a shady walnut tree. It is only a short stroll to **Scheggino** (280m, 1hr). The walk concludes at the village entrance, and a picnic on the river's edge can be enjoyed, alongside the levee to protect the settlement from flooding.

The flood level of the Nera at Scheggino

To reach the bus stop cross the modern bridge and walk out to the main road.

WALK 32
Monte Coscerno

Start/Finish	Gavelli
Distance	13km
Ascent/Descent	530m/530m
Difficulty	Grade 2
Walking time	3hr 30min
Maps	Monti di Spoleto e della Media Valnerina 1:25,000 SER
Refreshments	Bring picnic supplies with you as – drinking water apart – nothing is available at Gavelli.
Access	From Sant'Anatolia di Narco, turn off southeast for the 10km drive to Gavelli. At the village, park just off the road, alongside the bowling enclosure. No buses come up here.

This makes a wonderful day out, miles from anywhere. It wanders over superbly scenic 1683m Monte Coscerno, a colossally long, broad grassy ridge of limestone in upper Val di Narco. Apart from pockets of beech trees in protected hollows, it is windswept and bare, and home to twittering skylarks and birds of prey. It also provides perfect grassy grazing for sheep, cows, horses and donkeys – all presumably oblivious to the grandiose 360° views.

Waymarking is not abundant so follow directions and map carefully. The opening stretch is in common with a 'Sentiero della Transumanza', a route once taken by shepherds on their annual stock migrations.

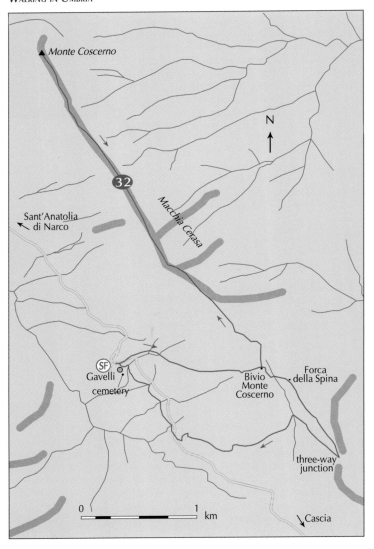

Gavelli, the walk start, is a peaceful **mountain hamlet** where life still revolves around livestock and the rhythms and seasons of the mountain. Many houses have stables set directly below the living area so as to exploit the natural heat generated by the animals.

The quiet hamlet of Gavelli

From **Gavelli** (1153m) walk up the road a short way to where a track breaks off left (E) signposted for the 'Sentiero della Transumanza', aka n.30. It quickly narrows to a clear path through light woodland and onto open rocky terrain studded with juniper shrubs, spiky eryngo flowers and aromatic herbs. With beautiful views over the upper valley, it follows a wire fence towards a conifer plantation. Here, stick to the edge of the trees to the signposted junction **Bivio Monte Coscerno** (1322m, 40min) overlooking pasture slopes. Fork left here – there is no path as such at first but head straight uphill (N) to gain the broad rocky crest that extends northwest. Despite the myriad tracks left by centuries of livestock, you cannot go wrong. Initially follow the wire fence in ascent to the 1500m mark. Here you join a rutted track past the

*The final leg back to
the village*

Macchia Cerasa, a surprisingly extensive beech copse
of artistically sculpted twisted branches that shelters on
the northern slopes. Needless to say the outlook is terrific
all the way. Minor downs alternate with longer ups as
you walk to the aerial-studded top of **Monte Coscerno**
(1683m, 1hr 20min). ◄

From here there is
a bird's-eye view
of Gavelli, and vast
outlook over the
cultivated plains
and wooded hills
of eastern Umbria,
the rugged Sibillini
Mountains and down
the Apennines to
Gran Sasso.

Return the same way to **Bivio Monte Coscerno**
(1322m) and proceed SE downhill on the lane to **Forca
della Spina** aka Fonte della Spina (1274m, 40min),
a broad saddle with drinking troughs and a bench.
Continue in the same direction on a lane coasting
through beech wood, forking right at a **three-way junction** (10min). Then it is leisurely descent NW-SW over
cultivated fields and flanking a sunny wall covered with
everlasting and globe flowers. The views back to Monte
Coscerno are both inspiring and satisfying. You cross the
road and proceed NW on a lane past the village **cemetery** and back to Gavelli (1153m, 50min).

WALK 33
Roccaporena to Cascia

Start/Finish	Roccaporena/Piazza Garibaldi, Cascia
Distance	6.5km
Descent	60m
Difficulty	Grade 2
Walking time	1hr 30min
Refreshments	Both villages have cafés and restaurants, and Cascia has groceries.
Public transport	Regular buses run between Cascia and Roccaporena.
Access	Roccaporena is a 6km drive from Cascia.

Set in a rocky amphitheatre, the tiny village of Roccaporena where the walk starts was the birthplace of Santa Rita, although Cascia takes most of the credit as the key years of her life were spent there. The devoted flock here pay homage at her house and vegetable garden, not to mention the 'Scoglio Sacro' (holy rock) where a chapel houses an oblong rock imprinted with the saint's elbows and knees.

The walk described here from Roccaparena to Cascia is also known as 'Sentiero Santa Rita', a pleasant stroll along the surprisingly steep-sided valley where the River Corno runs. After an opening length of tarmac, a path takes over. It has a stretch of railing, however, walkers should be aware that several sections are narrow and can feel a little exposed. The route is best avoided in bad weather due to the risk of rockfalls.

From the bus stop at **Roccaporena** (707m) walk down the road E, passing a route to the **Scoglio Sacro**. ▸ As you leave, look up left for the yawning natural rock cavity now known as the 'Grotta d'Oro', or the abode of the nymph-cum-oracle Porrina who gave her name to the village.

At first the road is overshadowed by sheer cliffs where birds of prey nest, while further on roofing protects from rock falls. After a bend near a ruined mill (Molinaccio), you fork right on a modern **bridge** over the **Fiume Corno** (25min) then immediately left with red/white waymarks.

This landmark 827m knoll has a stepped way leading to the top for wonderful views – allow 45min return.

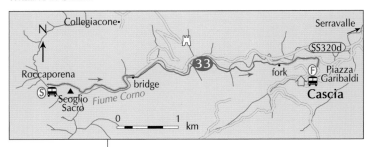

The old atmospheric way descends gently, passing tight against the mountainside. Sheltered corners host beech wood, sun-blasted slopes mean aromatic Mediterranean

The pleasant path above the river

herbs while the actual rockface is home to saxifrages. Soon ahead the slender Torre di Collegiacone stands out high on the heavily wooded mountain opposite, while below the poplar-lined river flows around fields.

As the valley opens up with immense views to the Sibillini Mountains northeast, the first buildings belonging to Cascia come into sight. At a fork in the path, go left downhill following the railing for steps to the road and a sign for 'Sentiero S Rita'. Branch right up the quiet tarmac below a singularly unsightly hotel, and into the town of **Cascia** on Via del Pago. Proceeding downhill, this forks right into Via XX Settembre, leading directly into the elongated main square **Piazza Garibaldi** (653m) lined with cafés and souvenir shops. The Tourist Office is at the opposite end, and the bus station only minutes downhill.

WALK 34

Monte Meraviglia

Start/Finish	San Sisto, Onelli
Distance	12.7km; or 10.2km
Ascent/Descent	650m/650m; or 250m/250m
Difficulty	Grade 2
Walking time	4hr; or 3hr
Maps	Monti Sibillini Cascia-Norcia sheet 666 1:50,000 Kompass (partial coverage)
Refreshments	Food and drinking water need to be carried; several *fontanelle* (drinking troughs) are touched on but they occasionally run dry. The Agriturismo on the shorter route has a restaurant (tel 0743 76819).
Public transport	A mid-morning bus from Cascia serves Onelli, but there are no afternoon runs so count on walking back to Cascia afterwards (via Casali San Antonio) or arrange to be picked up.
Access	From Cascia, take the SS471 (towards Monteleone) but turn off after 2.5km for Onelli – a further 3.5km. The church of San Sisto is on the far side of the quiet rural village; park there.

Monte Meraviglia (meaning 'wonder') on the outskirts of Cascia certainly lives up to its name as simply marvellous 360° views can be enjoyed from its 1392m summit. The walk entails a wonderful if tiring day out through quiet woodland and rural areas. There is no waymarking although clear lanes are followed throughout – with the notable exception of a 15min section of descent from the summit. A lower level variant is feasible without climbing to the summit, exiting via Casali San Antonio.

The church of San Sisto and Onelli with the Sibillini in the background

From the church of **San Sisto** at Onelli (953m) take the steep lane uphill SW, climbing quickly away from the village. Where the lane divides, take the fork left (S). The wide rocky way ascends steadily through light oak wood and sunny slopes of aromatic herbs, with vast views over uninhabited wooded hills. Near a saddle at the conclusion of the ascent stands the building **Casali Tetella** (1149m). Not far along a ruined stone farm is passed, then the lane bears WNW into the sheltered corridor of Valle Cucina. Gentle descent past fields and woodland below Monte Meraviglia will see you at the fascinating traditional albeit abandoned **Casale Franceschini** (1039m). Further on is the **Casale Luparini farm**, followed by a steady incline to a shoulder and a strategic

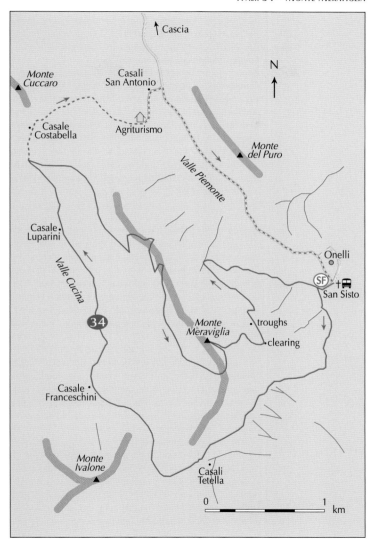

fork (978m, 1hr 45min). Unless you opt for the lower variant, turn right for the summit.

Lower variant via Casali San Antonio
Keep on in the same direction past nearby **Casale Costabella** to reach a fork with a concrete box structure. Turn right (E) here for the mostly level stretch in company with yellow 'Gasdotto' (gas pipeline) marker poles, past fields to views north to the Sibillini peaks. Further along the stony lane bears NE down past an **Agriturismo** to join a narrow surfaced road to **Casali San Antonio** (823m, 45min). From there you follow the 2.5km road right along **Valle Piemonte** for **Onelli** (30min). Otherwise for Cascia, turn left (3.5km).

The perfectly graded lane leads SE for the most part, swinging uphill in wide bends. Once out of the trees, the grassy slopes are studded with juniper shrubs and tiny flowers and home to twittering skylarks, not to mention grazing livestock in summer. You have ample time to appreciate the ever-improving panorama that initially embraces the long backbone of Monte Coscerno west-northwest, then takes in the rugged Terminillo south, and higher up the dramatic Gran Sasso and the long line-up of the Sibillini, true Apennines. But by this time you will have effortlessly gained the actual summit of **Monte Meraviglia** (1392m, 1hr 15min), near a landmark green repeater panel. Cascia is at your feet due north.

For the descent, cut down the grassy slope keeping on the right side of the panel, to where a faint track heads down left (NE) into beech wood. Moving NNE-SE it drops steeply to a pasture **clearing** (15min) where a clear lane left (N) begins. Not far along are watering **troughs** for livestock (1247m). Now the straightforward descent winds its way through oak and beech wood and the occasional clearing, not to mention a second set of drinking troughs. Swinging decidedly ESE it passes the fork where you turned off in ascent, returning to **San Sisto** and **Onelli** (45min).

6 NORCIA AND THE SIBILLINI

Bright mustard flowers in Valle Canatra (Walk 38)

INTRODUCTION

Autumn mist on the Piano Grande

In eastern Umbria a key town is elegant Norcia, birthplace of St Benedict, founder of the Benedictine monastic order no less. His statue keeps watch over the elegant central square. However, a close contender for pulling in visitors goes under the name of 'norcineria', the revered and noble art of sausage and salami making. Norcia also lies at the heart of world famous black truffle territory, celebrated in the annual winter Fiera del Tartufo. Foodie heaven!

It is a superb base for exploring the area, and has frequent buses from Spoleto, Rome and most other directions, not to mention full visitor facilities.

Running northwest from Norcia is sleepy Valle del Campiano. Who could imagine this rural backwater was at the apex of international medical fame in the 16th and 17th centuries? It all began at the abbey of Sant'Eutizio where the monks specialised in herbal medicine and cutting-edge surgery. Later forbidden to practice by ecclastical edict, they passed on their know-how to the inhabitants of nearby Preci, who perfected the art through practising on pigs. They were in great demand far and wide at the courts of emperors, sultans, and even Queen Elizabeth I. Walks 35, 36 and 37 visit the valley, which is served by buses from Norcia.

The valley doubles as the southeastern border of the Sibillini National Park, adjoining the Apennines. A highlight is the uniquely placed village of Castelluccio cluttered atop a conical hill. Legend attributes its settlement to a colony of Jews sent packing from Rome by Emperor Vespasian. With its permanent population down to 12, this wind-battered rural community survives on sheep herding and agriculture, boosted by tourism these days. It offers accommodation, rustic restaurants and a once-a-week bus link with Norcia (Thursday, for the market!), so a car can be helpful. Walk 38 begins here.

Dwarfed by soaring ridges and peaks, Castelluccio overlooks the marvellous and aptly named Piano Grande di Castelluccio located 1200m above sea level. Explored in Walk 39 the Piano Grande always puts on a good show. In wintertime snow covers the fields, transforming them into a huge cross-country ski arena; in the Middle Ages the church decreed that bells be rung in blizzards to guide travellers. In late spring, nature goes mad here. Almost overnight strips of arable land fields sown with lentils explode with wildflowers, akin to a watercolour painting streaked with vivid purple, yellow, red and crimson (mustard and cornflowers, poppies and vetch). This is the early June Fiorita (flowering), a significant challenge for photographers and bees alike! Walk 40 explores the southeastern corner of the Piano Grande, beginning at the Forca di Presta road pass near a hospitable refuge.

Note: Road and path maintenance along with infrastructure reconstruction is ongoing as damage from the 2016 earthquake is dealt with. The situation is in constant flux as improvements are made – check locally for the latest updates. Sibillini path conditions can be checked on www.sibillini.net.

Photogenic Campi Vecchio nestling on the hillside (Walk 36)

WALK 35
Preci and Sant'Eutizio

Start/Finish	Preci
Distance	9.7km
Ascent/Descent	520m/520m
Difficulty	Grade 1–2
Walking time	3hr
Maps	Monti Sibillini 1:25,000 SER
Refreshments	Borgo has grocery shops, while there are restaurants at Preci and alongside the abbey.
Public transport	Buses from Norcia serve Borgo and Preci (Mon–Sat).
Access	Preci is reached via the minor road SP476.
Note	Both Preci and Sant'Eutizio were damaged in the 2016 earthquake. Moreover, at the time of going to press, this route was obstructed just before San Marco and near Collescille so the complete walk may not be possible for the time being.

Beginning at the enchanting Umbrian village of Preci, this pleasant walk explores the lovely wooded and pastoral surrounds of Valle del Campiano. In common with a stretch of the Norcia–Narnia 'Sentiero benedettino' SB, the route drops through the hamlet of Borgo before traversing hillsides bright with wildflowers and lovely views. The destination is the fine Romanesque abbey of Sant'Eutizio, built into the hillside in a secluded valley and an inspiring place to visit. The return is made on little-frequented paths through woodland thick with the scent of Mediterranean plants.

Walking is straightforward but take extra care on the return stretch to Borgo as the path disappears for a little while. From the abbey, you can always return to Preci the same lovely way you came, or walk out to the main road (20min) and catch a bus back.

From the car park in upper Preci (596m) turn up alongside **Hotel agli Scacchi**, a 15th-century palace named after a prominent surgeon. In the peaceful pedestrian-only area amid historic buildings you walk downhill on paved Via Cavalotti to a lower parking area. Turn left then almost immediately right for a lane to **Borgo** (532m)

Preci is a beautiful spot to begin the walk

and the main road. Turn right (SE) for 5min to the end of the village and pass a **shrine** then left. This surfaced road soon reverts to a leafy lane E, which corresponds to n.501/SB.

At a concrete wall and **fork** (627m) keep right across **Valle Cascia** for the gentle climb out of beech wood onto open hillsides covered with masses of broom and wild orchids. Inspiring views range over the gently undulating hills and neighbouring farming valleys. At houses on a quiet road, turn left as the hamlet of **Collescille** becomes visible on a broom-splattered hillside. Soon after a picnic area, go right on a path for the nearby shrine of **San Marco** (850m, 1hr). Now a shady old path descends through oak to reach a narrow road then a belltower and cemetery. Here steep steps cut down a rockface to the beautiful premises of **Sant'Eutizio** (678m, 15min) in a jasmine-draped courtyard.

The **abbey** was founded in AD470 by San Spes (Sant'Eutizio was his follower) on a site occupied by cave-dwelling hermits. Sant'Eutizio was attributed

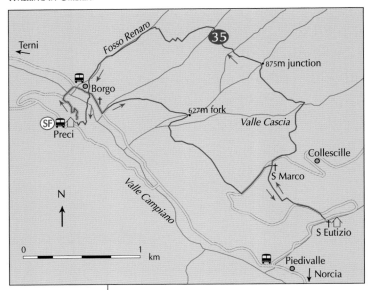

with miracle-making: during long dry periods when water shortages became dire, his belt would be carried in procession, and on the arrival at the monastery the heavens inevitably burst open.

Should you strike lucky and find the inner precincts open to the public, you will be able to inspect the ancient alchemist's laboratory as well as the collection of historical surgical instruments.

Afterwards walk back up to San Marco (850m, 20min) and go right towards Collescille. Not far along, below the actual hamlet, turn left on a stony way frequently used by sheep as your nose will tell you. At a patch of concrete paving with green metal poles, branch left (N) on a faint path through woodland but on the upper edge of a field. The path quickly widens and faint red paint marks appear on rocks (n.587 on maps). A lovely old route with the odd stretch of stone walling, it leads through holm oak wood

The scenic path to Sant'Eutizio

alternating with rocky sunny terrain with masses of aromatic herbs and broom. After a stream it bears NW on a level, cutting the SW flanks of Monte Moricone.

A short way after a lengthy collapsed stretch of walling (at approximately 875m), red stripes point you downhill on a steep rough track that ends in a field. (You have now well and truly left path n.587.) Follow the top edge of the field around to the right and shortly down to where a clear track resumes go right (NW) in steady descent. This feeds into a wider shady lane that sometimes doubles as a stream bed (lower **Fosso Renaro**) to reach Borgo (532m, 1hr 10min). On the opposite side of the road a path crosses a stream in the proximity of old channels constructed for the adjacent mill. An easy climb through woodland below the township emerges at a road, then it is not far back to the car park in upper **Preci** (596m, 15min).

WALK 36
Campi to Norcia

Start/Finish	Campi/Piazza San Benedetto, Norcia
Distance	9km
Ascent/Descent	360m/470m
Difficulty	Grade 1–2
Walking time	3hr
Maps	Monti Sibillini 1:25,000 SER
Refreshments	Picnics can be purchased at Campi. There are no cafés or restaurants until Norcia.
Public transport	Campi is served by Mon–Sat buses on the Norcia–Borgo Cerreto run.
Access	Campi is 12km north of Norcia. If travelling by car, it is more straightforward to park in Norcia and catch the bus to the walk start rather than the reverse; the bus stop is outside the café-grocery shop in Campi.
Note	At the time of going to press the route was obstructed between Campi and Capo del Colle – begin the walk at Capo del Colle.

This is a lovely and easy traverse from laidback Valle del Campiano across the Forca d'Ancarano pass and down to the beautiful walled town of Norcia. The walk shares the way with the 'Sentiero benedettino' route (from Narni to Norcia) 'SP'. A short section of the long-distance Sibillini ring route GAS (Grande Anello dei Sibillini), signed 'G' – is also followed. This region is fundamentally rural in character with cocks crowing, tractors at work in the fields and sheep grazing. En route, an exploratory detour is recommended into the picturesque hillside village of Campi Vecchio.

It is worth taking time to wander through the village.

From the bus stop at **Campi** (718m) leave the main road for the narrow surfaced road that climbs steeply NE past houses and the **Chiesa di San Antonio**. Continue uphill on n.501/SB past car parks for the final potholed metres to a T-junction near **Campi Vecchio** (875m, 20min). ◀

Fork right along the road but leave it almost immediately for the signed path left (in common with 'G') for

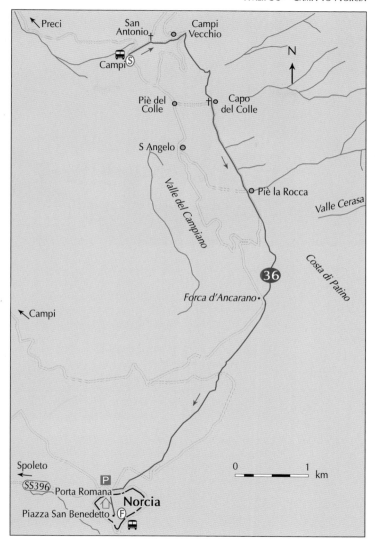

Capo del Colle surmounted by a ruins of a castle

a series of inclines and declines SSE between fields and predominantly oak woods with lovely views over the pastoral landscapes of **Valle del Campiano**. Follow red/white waymarking carefully at the many forks encountered. You part ways with 'G' at a fork and stick to n.501 to head S downhill onto alleyways between the tiny old houses and the beautifully frescoed church of San Antonio to the road at **Capo del Colle** (827m).

As you reach wash troughs branch left on Via Rossini to traverse the stretched-out settlement. The narrow surfaced road leads SSE into woodland high above the valley road. Take care not to miss the turn-off left for the lane coasting to **Piè la Rocca** (880m, 50min), a small square with benches and drinking water. A quiet surfaced road takes you uphill to where you are sent left onto a lane SE, climbing towards the base of Monte Patino. With sweeping views S to the vast Piano di Santa Scolastica, it is down to the road pass **Forca d'Ancarano** (1008m, 30min), where Walk 37 begins.

Without touching the tarmac, keep left on the initially faint path. Descending on a white rock base

Piazza San Benedetto in Norcia

through dry Mediterranean wood, this reveals enticing glimpses of walled Norcia below. Cross straight over the road for a lovely path lined with huge oak trees. Where this ends go right along a shady lane SSE, which touches on the road again but sticks to a lane. This leads through to the town walls where you go right to the nearby **Porta Romana** of Norcia. An appropriately grandiose arch, it opens onto pedestrian Corso Sertorio. Here your progress will undoubtedly be slowed as you pause to appreciate the mouth-watering displays of Norcineria and truffles. The walk concludes in the charming round **Piazza San Benedetto** (618m, 1hr 20min) in the company of a statue of the great saint himself.

WALK 37
Monte Patino

Start/Finish	Forca d'Ancarano
Distance	12.8km
Ascent/Descent	875m/875m
Difficulty	Grade 2
Walking time	5hr
Maps	Monti Sibillini 1:25,000 SER or Monti Sibillini Cascia-Norcia sheet 666 1:50,000 Kompass
Refreshments	Nothing en route so go equipped
Public transport	Mon–Sat buses on the Norcia–Borgo Cerreto run will let you off at the pass Forca d'Ancarano. Cars can be parked in a lane just off the road, taking care not to obstruct farm vehicles.
Note	At the time of going to press this route was closed to walkers until further notice.

This wonderfully varied loop walk takes you to belvedere extraordinaire Monte Patino with especially memorable views over the walled town of Norcia. It is easy to follow and takes clear paths beginning on pastureland and proceeding through woods up to open slopes that are ablaze with beautiful wildflowers at springtime. This area comes under the Sibillini National Park, and waymarking is a combination of park signs and CAI, and a brief stretch of the GAS (Grande Anello dei Sibillini).

Forca d'Ancarano is a key pass linking the Norcia plain with Valnerina, and it once hosted an ancient Etruscan site, although no traces are left today.

At **Forca d'Ancarano** (1008m) take the clear lane marked E14 that turns up NE between wheat fields bright with poppies and cornflowers. ◄ Only minutes along, at the first junction branch right, and past an old water trough. Not far on is a fork where you turn sharp left, leaving E14 and n.581. This steep rocky track (n.582) soon levels out as it heads N through light woodland. A gentle ascent ensues in the company of sweet broom shrubs and orchids; further on the way veers right (NE) into peaceful **Valle Cerasa**. Here stands of laburnum trees give way to clearings that are carpeted with bright wildflowers in spring. Your gaze will undoubtedly be drawn up right

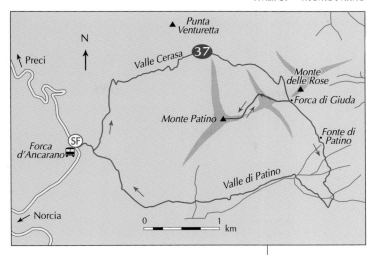

(southeast) to where Monte Patino looms opposite Punta Venturetta L (north). This green valley fold provides shelter for beech trees which grow up to the 1600m level, unusually high for this species. Above that the path climbs across open grassy slopes to join the GAS route below the rounded hummock of **Monte delle Rose**. A level stretch leads right (S) to the saddle **Forca di Giuda** (1794m, 2hr 15min).

Here ignore the GAS branch left and stick to n.582 as it forks sharp right for a lovely scenic coast due W. A minor col is touched on before the last leg up to the gigantic cross on the summit of **Monte Patino** (1883m, 25min). The reward is a fantastic bird's-eye view southwest over Norcia and its walls, and beyond to the cultivated plain in this southwestern corner of Umbria. The opposite direction means inspiring sight of the crests and peaks of the central Sibillini. A spot to be savoured.

Retrace your steps to Forca di Giuda (1794m, 20min) and turn right in preparation for a plunge on n.581/E14. Steepish at first it follows a fault of multi-coloured rock, traversing crumbly terrain. ▶ The gradient eases at **Fonte**

Watch your step here.

177

The huge summit cross on Monte Patino

di Patino (1557m), a spring with drinking troughs for livestock. A gentler path heads S through beech copses before swinging NW to join a broad gravel track in upper **Valle di Patino**, fragrant with broom and laburnum. Mostly W, it passes among rock outcrops and levels out. On the last leg it curves NW past an abandoned quarry and the forks encountered on the outward section. Keep left back to **Forca d'Ancarano** (1008m, 2hr).

WALK 38
Monte delle Rose

Start/Finish	Castelluccio di Norcia
Distance	13.8km
Ascent/Descent	665m/665m
Difficulty	Grade 2
Walking time	4hr 10min
Maps	Monti Sibillini 1:25,000 SER or Monti Sibillini Cascia-Norcia sheet 666 1:50,000 Kompass
Refreshments	Take a picnic from Castelluccio.
Public transport	The only bus runs from Norcia on Thu.
Access	Castelluccio can be reached by road from Norcia or Castelsantangelo sul Nera.
Note	Sadly, part of the old heart of Castelluccio was damaged in the 2016 earthquake.

After starting out at the fascinating hilltop hamlet of Castelluccio di Norcia, the opening stage of this lovely walk curves above the medium altitude pasture of Piano Perduto. The 'lost plain' was named after a bloody battle fought in 1522 (see below); nowadays colour comes from the dense concentrations of summer blooms – bright yellow mustard in the field of lentil crops and divine vivid pink peonies that flourish on the edge of woodland in little-visited Valle Canatra. Then there's pristine green – or russet in autumn – provided by the foliage of the magnificent beech trees on the mountain slopes, one of the few surviving ancient woods in the Sibillini, 1000 hectares in all.

This rewarding varied circuit is fairly straightforward although a compass is helpful in view of the lack of waymarking in places. Directions and map need to be followed carefully.

From **Castelluccio** (1452m) take the road N in the direction of Castelsantangelo. A short way along branch left onto an unmarked gravel lane. This rounds a corner through beech copses to enter **Valle Canatra** with good views over the medieval battlefield in **Piano Perduto**.

The '**lost plain**' was named after a terrible 1522 battle over land rights and the numerically superior

179

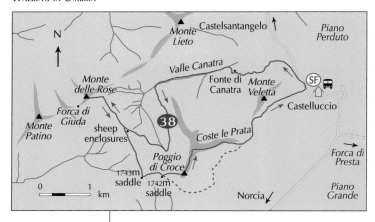

Norcians with 6000 men were pitted against a mere 600 soldiers from Visso in the north. However, as the tale goes, the latter called on their females to act as distraction – although exactly how can only be speculated upon. The ensuing massacre left the plain running red with blood.

Past grazing land is a picnic area and the drinking troughs of **Fonte di Canatra** (1360m, 30min). A clear lane proceeds W alongside fields, while ahead rises Monte delle Rose at the termination of this valley. Gradually, ever-thicker beech woods obscure the surrounding mountain flanks. At a conspicuous clearing used by woodcutters (1486m, 20min), turn left (S) uphill via a pretty shady side valley. The way narrows to a faint path, then climbs steadily to a lane. Turn right across open pasture, making your way gently uphill. Beautiful clumps of ancient beech gnarled are passed before **sheep enclosures** are reached on a broad crest. Here the well-marked GAS (Grande Anello dei Sibillini) is joined, albeit briefly. Continue NW together on a clear track, soon letting the GAS veer away left (for Forca di Giuda) – continue straight ahead. Around the 1750m mark, corresponding to the head of Val Canatra, leave the track and cut left

up the flowered slopes to the top of **Monte delle Rose** (1861m, 1hr 20min), marked by a large cairn. The marvellous outlook takes in the rolling hills of Umbria west, clad in dark woods, while from the opposite direction of this lookout are almost complete views of the Sibillini peaks and intermediate crests.

Castelluccio seen from the descent

Return to the track and the sheep enclosures and stick with the long-distance Grande Anello dei Sibillini (GAS) now, continuing SSW over stony-grassy slopes to an unnamed **1743m saddle**. Here you part ways with the trekking route and branch left (E) on faint path n.560 signed for 'Castelluccio'. ▶ At a **1742m saddle** (40min) a wide white lane is crossed.

Here you can see across the vast Piano Grande, with snow-spattered Monti della Laga in the distance, southeast. Closer, due east, is Poggio di Croce, your next destination, identifiable by what look like giant fingernail scratches.

Alternate route to Castelluccio (1hr)

This route, shorter by 20min, follows a straightforward lane SE at first below **Poggio di Croce** and gives ample time for admiring the vast expanse of the Piano Grande. Curving easily NE, it joins up with the main route to proceed to **Castelluccio**.

From the **1742m saddle** continue E on a faint lane which soon heads steeply uphill to the cairn and pole atop

Poggio di Croce (1883m, 20min) and great views. Then, with no path as such, head NNE along the flowered ridge-line to another pole on an unnamed 1850m peak for an even vaster outlook over the Piano Grande and a bird's-eye view of Castelluccio backed by the main Sibillini spine. After a short stretch NE along **Coste le Prata**, cut steeply downhill to the edge of beech woods and turn left onto the wide white lane encountered earlier. The last leg saunters below **Monte Veletta**, a popular launching point for hang-gliders. The walk concludes back at **Castelluccio** (1hr).

WALK 39
Piano Grande di Castelluccio

Start/Finish	Castelluccio di Norcia
Distance	15.5km
Ascent/Descent	200m/200m
Difficulty	Grade 1
Walking time	4hr (plus 20min for exploring the Mergani)
Maps	Monti Sibillini 1:25,000 SER or Monti Sibillini Cascia-Norcia sheet 666 1:50,000 Kompass
Refreshments	Castelluccio has some grocery shops as well as cafés and restaurants.
Public transport	The only bus runs from Norcia on Thursdays.
Access	Castelluccio can be reached by road from either Norcia or Castelsantangelo sul Nera.

Starting at landmark hilltop Castelluccio, this highly recommended loop wanders across the beautiful vast basin known as the Piano Grande, once home to a lake that disappeared underground during the Pleistocene era. Especially memorable in early June (known as the Fiorita) when the wildflowers and lentil fields are in full bloom, it is also fascinating in autumn with infinite shades of yellow and brown, and atmospheric mist. The walk route is slightly unclear in a couple of places but in good weather visual landmarks are abundant and progress straightforward; it mostly coincides with marked route E13.

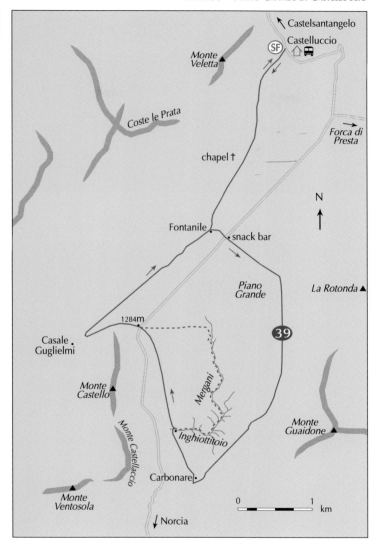

Castelluccio across the Piano Grande

Leave **Castelluccio** (1452m) on the rough lane alongside Albergo Sibilla. This descends gently SW-S to the plain. It passes between fields at the base of hills whose flanks are heavily scarred with centuries of spidery livestock tracks. A tiny **chapel** stands at the foot of a map of Italy of conifers planted by the Forestry Commission in the 1950s to celebrate an anniversary! The lane peters out as you approach a barbed wire fence – a rudimentary gate lets walkers through to the water troughs of **Fontanile** (1290m, 40min). Turn left here for the road and a camper van parking area with a summer **snack bar**. Cross over by a horse-riding enclosure and take the lane ESE marked E13/n.556, probably in the company of 4WDs transporting hang-gliders to the launching pads on nearby La Rotonda.

About 1km along you veer right (S) to traverse a vast uncultivated swathe of the Piano Grande, prairie-like here. Twittering winchats feeding on seeds in the knee-high grass can be deafening on this stretch, as can crickets and bees. Further on you link into a clearer track (SW) tracing the base of Monte Guaidone. Continue over a slight rise to follow a low embankment then head for the stone hut **Carbonare** (1272m), used by the charcoal burners of the past.

Now turn right (NNW) as far as the power line where a faint path takes you into a depression at the foot of an

outcrop beneath Monte Castellaccio for the **Inghiottitoio** (1257m, 1hr 30min).

At the Inghiottitoio

> The marvellously evocative Italian term *inghiottitoio* for sinkhole suggests gulping or swallowing. While the **sinkhole** itself is not that impressive – the opening is covered with wire netting – it is of key significance as this is where the water of the ancient lake disappeared underground.

Exploring the Mergani

It is worthwhile turning E to explore the natural drainage channels known as Mergani (from the Latin 'subside'). The grassy ditches are 3m wide and 20m deep, and crowded with clumps of reeds that provide wildlife with a handy hiding place. Foxes lurk in there, checking the progress of oblivious crows attracted in turn by the chance of a feast on the carcasses of reckless thirsty sheep who clamber into the ditches to drink then get stuck. With a vigilant eye out for marshy patches, follow the sheep paths parallel to the channel floor.

By keeping left at each ramification it is possible to cut across W to the **1284m point** on the roadside.

Up the other side of the depression you touch on a series of semi-circular dolinas, the result of karstification. A clear lane is joined leading N amid tiny gentians and pretty narcissus to the **1284m point** on roadside (20min).

Now a clear lane used by shepherds heads W into a side valley at the foot of Monte Castello, and on towards drinking troughs at ruined hut **Casale Guglielmi** (1309m). However, a tad before the structure turn right (NE) on the faint lane at the base of terraced slopes to return to the **Fontanile** (1284m, 45min) encountered earlier on. Then return to **Castelluccio** (1452m, 45min).

WALK 40
Dogana Loop

Start/Finish	Forca di Presta
Distance	15.5km
Ascent/Descent	430m/430m
Difficulty	Grade 1–2
Walking time	4hr
Maps	Monti Sibillini 1:25,000 SER or Monti Sibillini Cascia-Norcia sheet 666 1:50,000 Kompass
Refreshments	Near Forca di Presta is friendly old-style Rifugio degli Alpini for meals and snacks, while Colle Le Cese also has a good restaurant.
Access	The road pass Forca di Presta is an 8km drive from Castelluccio, or 30km from Norcia. No buses come this way.

A wonderful circuit in the southeastern corner of the renowned Piano Grande di Castelluccio, this takes in the pretty and little visited Dogana and Piano Piccolo offshoots. The outward stretch uses a fragment of the long-distance GAS (Grande Anello dei Sibillini) via a succession of scenic ridges with far-reaching views to the Monti della Laga that spread over neighbouring Lazio and Abruzzo. And there are memorable vistas over the vastness of the Piano Grande itself, inspiring at any time of year.

Forca di Presta is believed to have gotten its **name** from either *prestito* for 'loan', referring to ancient land leasing practises, or *praesto* for 'a place high up'. 'Dogana' on the other hand means 'customs', in this case denoting a valley close to the old border between the Kingdom of Naples and the Papal States.

From **Forca di Presta** (1534m) set out along the lane due S, signed for the GAS. Only a short walk away is **Rifugio degli Alpini**. Continue in gentle ascent on the

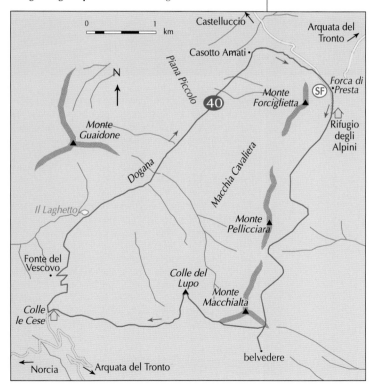

At the belvedere and Monte Vettore

broad gravel track across bare pastureland skirting Monte Pellicciara. Not far on where the track bears W, take the short detour left along a wooden walkway to a **belvedere** where helpful photo panels identify mountain ranges near and far.

Back on the wide track proceed due W beneath Monte Macchialta. Where a corner is rounded watch out for the faintly marked path right (NW) uphill over karstic terrain. A modest rise is reached with stunning views over the Piano Grande and hilltop Castelluccio, not to mention the central Sibillini peaks. At **Colle del Lupo** (col of the wolf) (1610m) turn left (SSW) onto a lane back into beech wood and soon onto broad scenic crests. Then it is W to the broad saddle and low-key ski area of **Colle le Cese** (1484m, 2hr) and its *rifugio*. Close to the building take the clear lane (n.557) N through beech, descending in curves to the broad pasture valley known as **Dogana**. At **Fonte del Vescovo** (bishop's spring) drinking troughs it bears NE in the shade of the gentle slopes of Monte Guaidone.

Not far along is diminutive **Il Laghetto** (little lake) (1370m), with rushes, water fowl and frogs galore, along

with a curious silo. Now an orange earth track leads along the broad Dogana trough, at the far end of which rises the unmistakable Redentore-Vettore massif. Close at hand east the mountain flanks are carpeted by the Macchia Cavaliera beech wood, a mere fragment of the ancient forest that once covered the entire Piano Grande. The bare ridge above it is a favourite launching pad for hang gliders. As the valley and track bear left into **Piano Piccolo**, take care not to miss the fainter lane right (red/white marker), still NE. Accompanied by skylarks and swallows and pretty thrift flowers, the way proceeds to ruined **Casotto Amati** (1373m). Soon afterwards leave the lane for a path right (E) uphill below the road at the foot of Monte Vettoretto. The tarmac is joined very briefly as you climb past a spring spouting deliciously cool water, to arrive back at **Forca di Presta** (1534m, 2hr), and the walk's end.

Perfectly formed Il Laghetto

189

APPENDIX A
Route summary table

No	Start/Finish	Distance	Grade	Time	Page
1 ALTA VAL TIBERINA, GUBBIO AND MONTE CUCCO					
1	Monte Santa Maria Tiberina	10km	1–2	3hr	30
2	Montone	8.2km	2	2hr 15min	33
3	Montone	15km	2	4hr 15min	37
4	Migiana di Monte Tezio	12km	2	3hr 30min	41
5	Gubbio	7km	2	2hr 45min	44
6	Gubbio	11km	2	3hr	48
7	Decollo Sud car park, Monte Cucco	6.2km	2–3	2hr 30min	53
8	Val di Rio Freddo, Monte Cucco	8.5km	1–2	3hr 20min	56
2 LAGO TRASIMENO AND ENVIRONS					
9	Ca' di Giano, Tuoro	12km	1–2	2hr 45min	62
10	Passignano	15km	2	3hr 40min	66
11	Isola Maggiore	2.5km	1	1hr 10min	69
12	Isola Polvese	3.5km	1	1hr	72

No	Start/Finish	Distance	Grade	Time	Page
13	Montemelino	6.5km	2	2hr 10min	74
14	Paciano	11km	2	3hr	78
15	Montarale park, Montarale	13km	2	3hr	82
3 ORVIETO AND TODI					
16	Orvieto	6km	1	1hr 45min	88
17	Orvieto	6km	1–2	2hr	91
18	Orvieto/Bolsena	15.6km	2	4hr	94
19	Titignano	13.5km	2–3	4hr 30min	99
20	Titignano	7km	1	2hr	102
21	Civitella del Lago	11km	2	3hr 30min	104
22	Todi/Pontecuti	4.3km	1	1hr	108
23	Vasciano	17km	1–2	4hr 30min	111
4 ASSISI AND AROUND					
24	Bettona	17km	2–3	5hr 10min	117
25	Assisi	14.3	2–3	5hr	121
26	Spello	12.3km	2	3hr 45min	125

No	Start/Finish	Distance	Grade	Time	Page
27	Bevagna/Montefalco	13km	1–2	3hr 30min	130
5 SPOLETO AND THE VALNERINA					
28	Spoleto	10.5km	1–2	3hr 45min	138
29	Spoleto	5.2km	1	1hr 20min	143
30	Spoleto/Sant'Anatolia di Narco	19km	1–2	5hr 15min	147
31	Valle di Nera	8.6km	1	2hr 15min	152
32	Gavelli	13km	2	3hr 30min	155
33	Roccaporena/Cascia	6.5km	2	1hr 30min	159
34	Onelli	12.7km	2	4hr	161
6 NORCIA AND THE SIBILLINI					
35	Preci	9.7km	1–2	3hr	168
36	Campi/Norcia	9km	1–2	3hr	172
37	Forca d'Ancarano	12.8km	2	5hr	176
38	Castelluccio di Norcia	13.8km	2	4hr 10min	179
39	Castelluccio di Norcia	15.5km	1	4hr	182
40	Forca di Presta	15.5km	1–2	4hr	186

APPENDIX B
Italian–English Glossary

Useful general expressions

Grazie	Thank you
Prego	You're welcome
Quanto costa?	How much is that?
Posso pagare con	
la carta di credito?	Can I pay by credit card?

For exploring

abbazia	abbey
acquedotto	water supply, aqueduct
agriturismo	farm with meals and accommodation
albergo	hotel
alimentari	grocery shop
andata/ritorno (a/r)	return trip
anello	ring
ascensore	lift
autostazione	bus station
belvedere	viewpoint
biglietteria	ticket office
biglietto	ticket
bivio	junction
borgo	village or town
casale/casali	farm house/ houses
castello	castle
chiesa	church
collina	hill

comune, municipio	council, town hall
convento, monastero	convent, monastery
croce	cross
divieto di accesso	no entry
divieto di caccia	no hunting
duomo	cathedral
edicola, maestà	shrine
eremo	hermitage
fermata bus	bus stop
ferrovia	railway line
fiume	river
fontana, fontanella, fonte	fountain, spring,
forca	pass, saddle
forra/forro	canyon
fortezza, rocca	fortress
fosso	gully, water course, trench
frazione, vocabolo	hamlet
galleria	tunnel
giardino	garden
giro	loop walk
gola, gole, voragine	canyon
grotta	cave
guado	ford
imbarcadero, imbarco traghetto, pontile	ferry landing stage
incrocio	intersection
isola	island
lago	lake
molino, mulino (a vento)	(wind) mill
monte	mountain

museo	museum
ometto	literally 'little man', cairn path marker
ostello	hostel
panificio, fornaio	bakery
percorso	route
percorso meccanizzato, scala mobile	escalator
pernottamento	overnight stay
piazza	town square
podere, tenuta	rural property
poggio	knoll
ponte	bridge
porta	door, gateway
pozzo	well
Pro Loco	Tourist Info
quartiere	town district
rio, torrente	mountain stream
rocca	fortress, tower
rudere	ruin
rupe	steep-sided rock platform
santuario	sanctuary, church
scoglio	cliff, outcrop
sentiero	path
sosta	(literally 'rest'), point of interest
spuntino	snack
stazione ferroviaria	railway station
sterrata	unsurfaced road, lane
strada	surfaced road
strada senza uscita	dead end road
torre	tower

APPENDIX C
Useful contacts

When calling an Italian landline number always include the initial zero. On the other hand numbers beginning with '3' are mobiles and need to be dialled as stand (ie without a zero). If ringing from overseas preface all Italian telephone numbers with +39.

Tourist information

Italian State Tourist Board
www.enit.it

Tourist offices in Umbria
The umbrella web site www.umbriatourism.it covers most offices.

Assisi
Tel 075 8138680

Bevagna
Tel 0742 361667
www.prolocobevagna.it

Cascia
Tel 0743 71147
www.lavalnerina.it

Castiglione del Lago
Tel 075 9652484/075 9652738

Città di Castello
Tel 075 8554922

Foligno
Tel 0742 354459/0742 354165

Gubbio
Tel 075 9220693

Montefalco
Tel 0742 616127
www.montefalcodoc.it

Norcia
Tel 0743 828173
www.lavalnerina.it

Tel 349 8838049/328 1797616
www.prolocorcia.it

Orvieto
Tel 0763 341772

Passignano sul Trasimeno
Tel 075 0440043

Perugia
Tel 075 5736458/075 5772686

Spoleto
Tel 0743 218621

Todi
Tel 075 8956227

Umbertide
Tel 075 9417099

Accommodation

Assisi
Hotel Posta Panoramic
www.hotelpostassisi.it
Tel 075 812558

Bettona
B&B La Piazzetta
www.bbpiazzetta.it
Tel 333 9892335

Bevagna
Chiostro di Bevagna
www.ilchiostrodibevagna.com
Tel 0742 361987

Cascia
Minihotel La Tavernetta
www.minihotellatavernetta.com
Tel 0743 71387

Agriturismo Casale S. Antonio
www.casalesantantonio.it
Tel 0743 76819

Castelluccio
Locanda de' Senari
www.agriturismosenari.it
Tel 0743 821205

Castel San Felice
Abbazia Santi Felice e Mauro
www.abbazia.net
Tel 0743 613427

Castiglione del Lago
Hotel La Torre
Tel 075 951666
www.latorretrasimeno.com

Città di Castello
Hotel Umbria
www.hotelumbria.net
Tel 075 8554925

Civitella del Lago
Casetta di Gloria
Tel 340 6517082

Collemancio
Il Rientro
www.ilrientro.com
Tel 0742 72420

Forca di Presta
Rifugio degli Alpini
Tel 347 0875331

Gubbio
Residenza Le Logge
www.residencegubbio.it
Tel 075 9277574

Isola Maggiore
Da Sauro
www.dasauro.it
Tel 075 826168

Isola Polvese
Fattoria Il Poggio
www.fattoriaisolapolvese.com
Tel 075 9659550

Monte Cucco
Albergo Monte Cucco 'Da Tobia'
www.albergomontecucco.it
Tel 075 9177194

Rifugio Valletta
Tel 338 1863355

Montefalco
Hotel Ororosso
Tel 0742 378829
www.ororossohotel.it

Monteluco
Albergo Ferretti
Tel 0743 49849
www.albergoferretti.com

Montone
Hotel Fortebraccio
www.hotelfortebraccio.it
Tel 075 9306400

Locanda del Capitano
www.ilcapitano.com
Tel 075 9603521

Norcia
Il Capisterium Hostel
www.norciaospitalita.it
Tel 349 3002091

Norcia hotels
www.bianconi.com
Tel 0743 816513

Orvieto
Villa Mercede B&B
villamercede@orvienet
Tel 0763 341766

Passignano sul Trasimeno
Hotel Lido
www.hotellidoperugia.com
Tel 075 827219

Perugia
Primavera Mini Hotel
Tel 075 5721657
www.primaveraminihotel.it

Pesciano
Agriturismo I Rossi
www.ilmerollo.com
Tel 075 8947079

Piegaro
Ca' de' Principi
www.dimorastorica.it
Tel 075 8358040

Da Elio
www.daelio.it
Tel 075 8358005

Scheggino
Hotel del Ponte
www.hoteldelpontescatolini.it
Tel 0743 61253

Spello
Hotel il Cacciatore
www.ilcacciatorehotel.com
Tel 0742 301603

Spoleto
Albergo Panciolle
www.ilpanciolle.it
Tel 0743 45677

Titignano
Castello di Titignano
www.titignano.it

Todi
Fawlty Towers
Tel 333 4931471
www.fawltytowersrooms.com

Umbertide
Hotel Capponi
Tel 075 9412662
www.hotelcapponi.com

Vallo di Nera
Locanda Cacio Re
www.caciore.com
Tel 0743 617003

Transport

Getting to Umbria
Ancona airport,
www.aeroportomarche.it

Perugia airport,
www.airport.umbria.it.

Pescara airport,
www.abruzzoairport.com.

Pisa airport,
www.pisa-airport.com

Rome's airports – Fiumicino, www.adr.it/fiumicino, and Ciampino, www.adr.it/ciampino

Long-distance coaches, www.sulga.eu

Getting around Umbria
The centralised network, Umbria Mobilità, www.umbriamobilita.it

Rail companies
Trenitalia (www.trenitalia.it, tel 892021) and FCU (see Umbria Mobilità above)

Useful websites
www.montideltezio.it for more routes on Monte Tezio

www.discovermontecucco.it for more routes and other activities in the Monte Cucco regional park

www.grottamontecucco.umbria.it for information on the cave located on the mountain's northern edge, visitable with a guide

www.nelleterredeltrasimeno.com has an array of further walking routes in the environs of Lago Trasimeno

www.parks.it/parco.fluviale.tevere for the Lago di Corbara area which comes under the Parco Fluviale del Tevere

www.parks.it/parco.monte.subasio for more information and walk routes on Monte Subasio

https://ripartiredaisentieri.cai.it for suggestions of safe routes in the areas affected by the 2016 earthquake (in Italian)

www.sibillini.net (and see Cicerone's *Italy's Sibillini National Park*) for more walks in the area, including the multi-day trek Grande Anello dei Sibillini

Via Francigena
The Via Francigena pilgrim route, indicated by blue/yellow paint stripes, passes through Umbria. See Cicerone's two-volume *The Via Francigena: Canterbury to Rome*, for more about this European Cultural Itinerary.

Walking along the Dogana trough (Walk 40)

IF YOU ENJOYED THIS GUIDEBOOK YOU MIGHT ALSO BE INTERESTED IN...

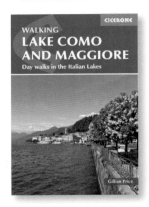

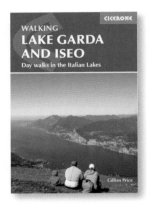

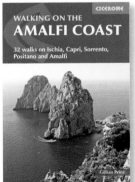

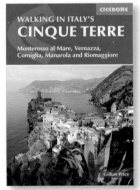

Available August 2019

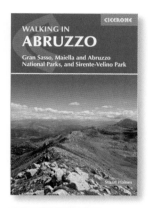
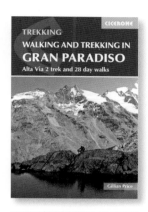
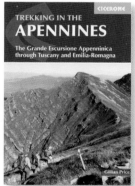
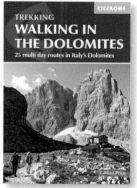

The Great
Outdoors

DIGITAL EDITIONS
30-DAY
FREE TRIAL

- Substantial savings on the newsstand price and print subscriptions
- Instant access wherever you are, even if you are offline
- Back issues at your fingertips

Downloading **The Great Outdoors** to your digital device is easy, just follow the steps below:

1 **Download the App** from the App Store

2 **Open the App**, click on 'subscriptions' and choose an annual subscription

3 **Download** the latest issue and enjoy

Available on the
App Store

The digital edition is also available on

The 30-day free trial is not available on Android or Pocketmags and is only available to new subscribers

Available on
Android

pocketmags.com

LISTING OF CICERONE GUIDES

SCOTLAND

Backpacker's Britain:
    Northern Scotland
Ben Nevis and Glen Coe
Cycling in the Hebrides
Great Mountain Days in Scotland
Mountain Biking in Southern and
    Central Scotland
Mountain Biking in West and
    North West Scotland
Not the West Highland Way
Scotland
Scotland's Best Small Mountains
Scotland's Mountain Ridges
Scrambles in Lochaber
The Ayrshire and Arran Coastal Paths
The Border Country
The Borders Abbeys Way
The Cape Wrath Trail
The Great Glen Way
The Great Glen Way Map Booklet
The Hebridean Way
The Hebrides
The Isle of Mull
The Isle of Skye
The Skye Trail
The Southern Upland Way
The Speyside Way
The Speyside Way Map Booklet
The West Highland Way
Walking Highland Perthshire
Walking in Scotland's Far North
Walking in the Angus Glens
Walking in the Cairngorms
Walking in the Ochils, Campsie Fells
    and Lomond Hills
Walking in the Pentland Hills
Walking in the Southern Uplands
Walking in Torridon
Walking Loch Lomond and
    the Trossachs
Walking on Arran
Walking on Harris and Lewis
Walking on Rum and the Small Isles
Walking on the Orkney and
    Shetland Isles
Walking on Uist and Barra
Walking the Corbetts
    Vol 1 South of the Great Glen
Walking the Corbetts
    Vol 2 North of the Great Glen
Walking the Munros
    Vol 1 – Southern, Central and
    Western Highlands
Walking the Munros
    Vol 2 – Northern Highlands and
    the Cairngorms

West Highland Way Map Booklet
Winter Climbs Ben Nevis and
    Glen Coe
Winter Climbs in the Cairngorms

NORTHERN ENGLAND TRAILS

Hadrian's Wall Path
Hadrian's Wall Path Map Booklet
Pennine Way Map Booklet
The Coast to Coast Map Booklet
The Coast to Coast Walk
The Dales Way
The Dales Way Map Booklet
The Pennine Way

LAKE DISTRICT

Cycling in the Lake District
Great Mountain Days in the
    Lake District
Lake District Winter Climbs
Lake District: High Level and
    Fell Walks
Lake District: Low Level and
    Lake Walks
Mountain Biking in the Lake District
Outdoor Adventures with Children –
    Lake District
Scrambles in the Lake District –
    North
Scrambles in the Lake District –
    South
Short Walks in Lakeland
    Book 1: South Lakeland
Short Walks in Lakeland
    Book 2: North Lakeland
Short Walks in Lakeland
    Book 3: West Lakeland
The Cumbria Way
Tour of the Lake District
Trail and Fell Running in the
    Lake District

NORTH WEST ENGLAND
AND THE ISLE OF MAN

Cycling the Pennine Bridleway
Cycling the Way of the Roses
Isle of Man Coastal Path
The Lancashire Cycleway
The Lune Valley and Howgills
The Ribble Way
Walking in Cumbria's Eden Valley
Walking in Lancashire
Walking in the Forest of Bowland
    and Pendle
Walking on the Isle of Man
Walking on the West Pennine Moors
Walks in Ribble Country
Walks in Silverdale and Arnside

NORTH EAST ENGLAND,
YORKSHIRE DALES
AND PENNINES

Cycling in the Yorkshire Dales
Great Mountain Days in
    the Pennines
Mountain Biking in the
    Yorkshire Dales
South Pennine Walks
St Oswald's Way and
    St Cuthbert's Way
The Cleveland Way and the
    Yorkshire Wolds Way
The Cleveland Way Map Booklet
The North York Moors
The Reivers Way
The Teesdale Way
Trail and Fell Running in the
    Yorkshire Dales
Walking in County Durham
Walking in Northumberland
Walking in the North Pennines
Walking in the Yorkshire Dales:
    North and East
Walking in the Yorkshire Dales:
    South and West
Walks in Dales Country
Walks in the Yorkshire Dales

WALES AND WELSH BORDERS

Cycling Lôn Las Cymru
Glyndwr's Way
Great Mountain Days in Snowdonia
Hillwalking in Shropshire
Hillwalking in Wales – Vol 1
Hillwalking in Wales – Vol 2
Mountain Walking in Snowdonia
Offa's Dyke Map Booklet
Offa's Dyke Path
Ridges of Snowdonia
Scrambles in Snowdonia
The Ascent of Snowdon
The Ceredigion and Snowdonia
    Coast Paths
The Pembrokeshire Coast Path
Pembrokeshire Coast Path
    Map Booklet
The Severn Way
The Snowdonia Way
The Wales Coast Path
The Wye Valley Walk
Walking in Carmarthenshire
Walking in Pembrokeshire
Walking in the Forest of Dean
Walking in the South Wales Valleys
Walking in the Wye Valley
Walking on the Brecon Beacons
Walking on the Gower

For full information on all our guides,
books and eBooks, visit our website:
www.cicerone.co.uk

Walking – Trekking – Mountaineering – Climbing – Cycling

Over 50 years, Cicerone have built up an outstanding collection of over 300 guides, inspiring all sorts of amazing adventures.

Every guide comes from extensive exploration and research by our expert authors, all with a passion for their subjects. They are frequently praised, endorsed and used by clubs, instructors and outdoor organisations.

All our titles can now be bought as **e-books**, **ePubs** and **Kindle** files and we also have an online magazine – **Cicerone Extra** – with features to help cyclists, climbers, walkers and trekkers choose their next adventure, at home or abroad.

Our website shows any **new information** we've had in since a book was published. Please do let us know if you find anything has changed, so that we can publish the latest details. On our **website** you'll also find great ideas and lots of detailed information about what's inside every guide and you can buy **individual routes** from many of them online.

It's easy to keep in touch with what's going on at Cicerone by getting our monthly **free e-newsletter**, which is full of offers, competitions, up-to-date information and topical articles. You can subscribe on our home page and also follow us on **Facebook** and **Twitter** or dip into our **blog**.

Cicerone – the very best guides for exploring the world.

CICERONE

Juniper House, Murley Moss, Oxenholme Road, Kendal, Cumbria LA9 7RL
Tel: 015395 62069 info@cicerone.co.uk
www.cicerone.co.uk